National Wildlife Federation

RANGER RICK'S SURPRISE BOOK

SURPRISES FROM AGES PAST

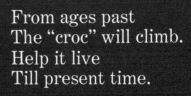

From ages past
The "croc" will climb.
Help it live
Till present time.

PROTECTED AREA

CROC SHOP

BAKERY

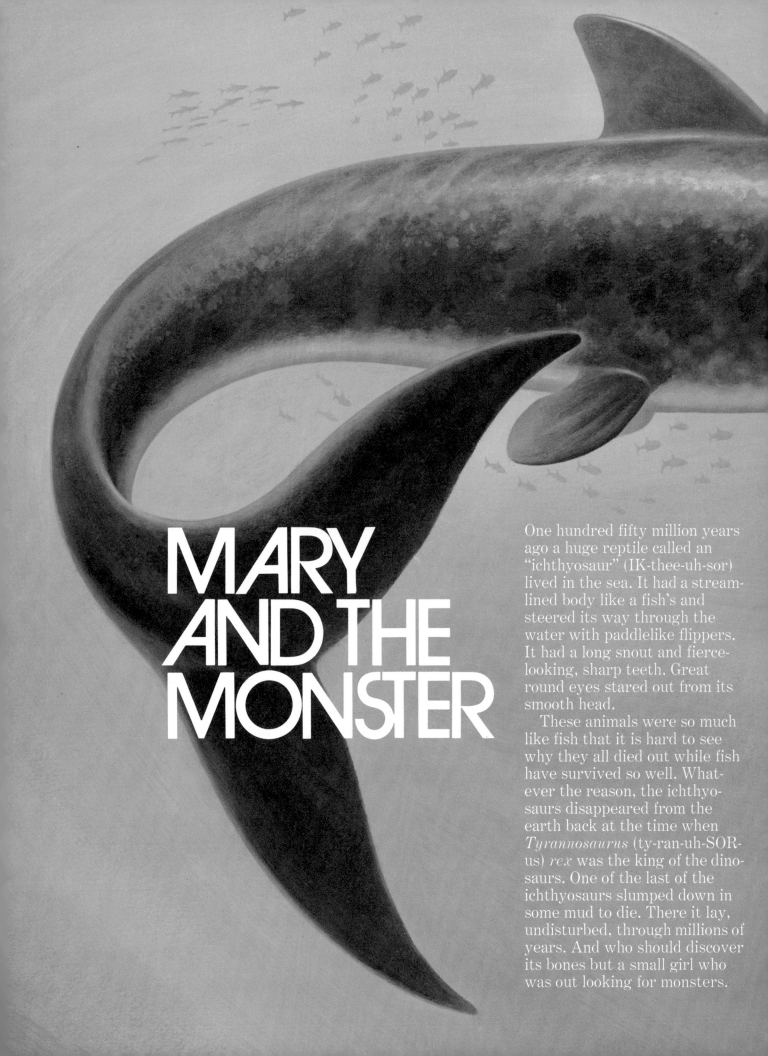

MARY AND THE MONSTER

One hundred fifty million years ago a huge reptile called an "ichthyosaur" (IK-thee-uh-sor) lived in the sea. It had a streamlined body like a fish's and steered its way through the water with paddlelike flippers. It had a long snout and fierce-looking, sharp teeth. Great round eyes stared out from its smooth head.

These animals were so much like fish that it is hard to see why they all died out while fish have survived so well. Whatever the reason, the ichthyosaurs disappeared from the earth back at the time when *Tyrannosaurus* (ty-ran-uh-SOR-us) *rex* was the king of the dinosaurs. One of the last of the ichthyosaurs slumped down in some mud to die. There it lay, undisturbed, through millions of years. And who should discover its bones but a small girl who was out looking for monsters.

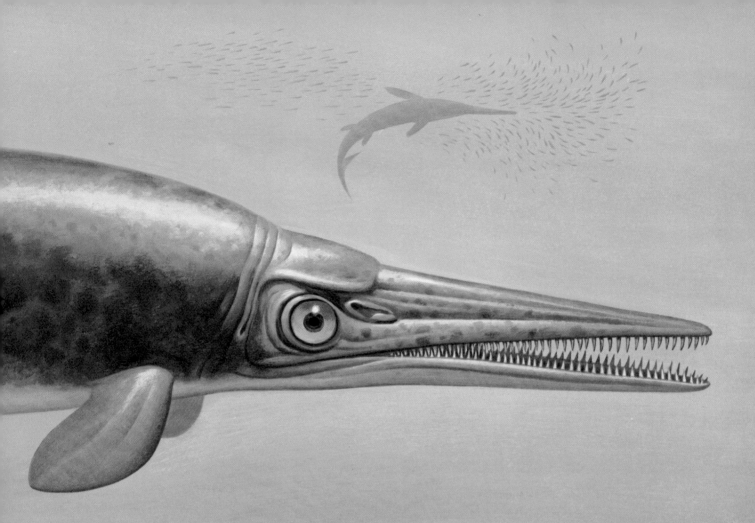

The story begins over one hundred fifty years ago beside the same seas where the ichthyosaurs had roamed. In the small town of Lyme Regis, on the south coast of England, lived the Anning family. Mr. Anning had been a carpenter. Although they had never been rich, there had always been enough money to manage on. Since her husband had died the year before, Mrs. Anning had had a hard time supporting her two children, Mary and Joseph.

One day Mrs. Anning went to the door and called, "Mary."

There was no answer.

"Where's that girl gone now?" she asked.

"I don't know, Mama," answered Joseph.

"She's down at the cliff, isn't she?" asked Mrs. Anning, in a cross voice. "Haven't I said she's to waste no more time poking about those cliffs? She's 12 years old and does nothing around the house."

"We've found something good this time, Mama," said Joseph in a whisper.

"Something good, indeed!" Mrs. Anning answered angrily. "It will just be more rubbish and clutter like this!"

As she spoke she knocked a large fossil onto the flagstone floor. It broke, and part of it rolled under a chair. Joseph dived after it and gathered up the pieces. He tried to fit them together again.

"That's an ammonite (AM-uh-nite), Mama," cried Joseph. "We could have sold it."

"Who'd pay for a worthless bit of stone?" asked his mother.

"Pa used to sell them for us in the shop," said Joseph.

"No one comes to the shop now," said his mother, and her mouth closed in a tight line.

When Mr. Anning was alive he had encouraged the children to look for shells and bones along the cliffs. Mary, with her sharp eyes and clever fingers, could pry ammonites right out of the rock. Mr. Anning told his customers about these curios from the past, and often they would give Mary a penny or two in exchange for a fossil.

Now no one came to the empty shop, and the piles of fossils gathered dust. But Mary could not stay away from the cliffs. Finding pieces of history was all she wanted to do.

Mary didn't come home until after dark that night. She had

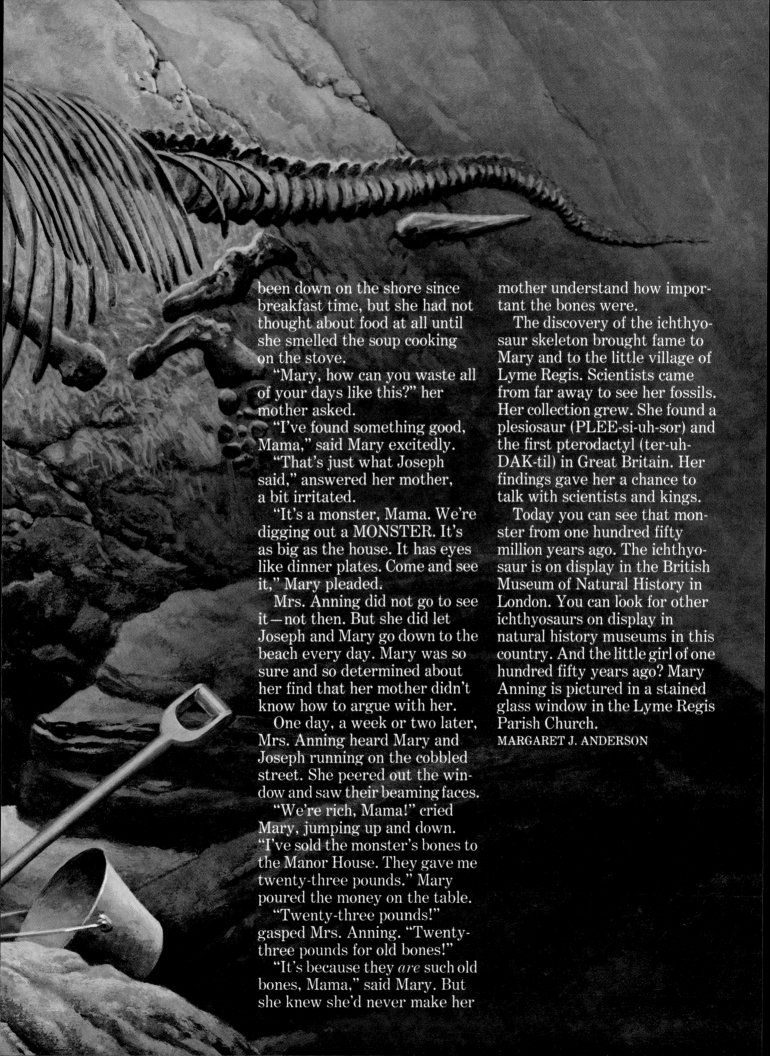

been down on the shore since breakfast time, but she had not thought about food at all until she smelled the soup cooking on the stove.

"Mary, how can you waste all of your days like this?" her mother asked.

"I've found something good, Mama," said Mary excitedly.

"That's just what Joseph said," answered her mother, a bit irritated.

"It's a monster, Mama. We're digging out a MONSTER. It's as big as the house. It has eyes like dinner plates. Come and see it," Mary pleaded.

Mrs. Anning did not go to see it—not then. But she did let Joseph and Mary go down to the beach every day. Mary was so sure and so determined about her find that her mother didn't know how to argue with her.

One day, a week or two later, Mrs. Anning heard Mary and Joseph running on the cobbled street. She peered out the window and saw their beaming faces.

"We're rich, Mama!" cried Mary, jumping up and down. "I've sold the monster's bones to the Manor House. They gave me twenty-three pounds." Mary poured the money on the table.

"Twenty-three pounds!" gasped Mrs. Anning. "Twenty-three pounds for old bones!"

"It's because they *are* such old bones, Mama," said Mary. But she knew she'd never make her mother understand how important the bones were.

The discovery of the ichthyosaur skeleton brought fame to Mary and to the little village of Lyme Regis. Scientists came from far away to see her fossils. Her collection grew. She found a plesiosaur (PLEE-si-uh-sor) and the first pterodactyl (ter-uh-DAK-til) in Great Britain. Her findings gave her a chance to talk with scientists and kings.

Today you can see that monster from one hundred fifty million years ago. The ichthyosaur is on display in the British Museum of Natural History in London. You can look for other ichthyosaurs on display in natural history museums in this country. And the little girl of one hundred fifty years ago? Mary Anning is pictured in a stained glass window in the Lyme Regis Parish Church.

MARGARET J. ANDERSON

LIVING FOSSILS

Imagine yourself in a very strange forest. It is hard for you to move around, because the forest is thick and swampy and has no trails. Suddenly you see something familiar, a dragonfly. But it has a wingspan longer than your outstretched arms! You watch the creature fly slowly, silently past another familiar sight—a fern. But the fern is a giant too, taller than your house.

of the *horsetails* you find in the woods look a lot like their ancestors. But they are only about knee-high. Imagine them as tall as oak trees! There were many that size growing in thick clumps in ancient swamps.

Club mosses (1) are another modern relative of the prehistoric giants. These small, green plants creep or trail over the ground. Sometimes they are called ground pines, because

changed very little since then. Flat, ribbonlike *liverworts* (3) are also unchanged. They still grow on moist rocks, along wet stream banks and in swamps. Unlike most other plants that live on land, liverworts have no roots, stems or leaves.

One giant, the *tree fern* (4), still grows as large as it did in prehistoric times. Reaching up to 60 feet high, these huge ferns thrive in the warm, moist

A fantasy land? No—such forests existed 300 million years ago, even before the dinosaurs!

What happened to those ancient forests? The warm, wet climate changed to a cooler, drier one. Many plants, such as giant club mosses and horsetails, did not survive, but their smaller relatives continued to live.

Today you can see many of these "living fossils" on the forest floor. For example, most

they look like little pine trees with scaly bark. Their branches stick up in the air only 5 to 20 centimeters (2 to 8 in.). These club mosses are miniature versions of prehistoric club moss trees, which sometimes grew as high as a ten-story building.

Not all "living fossils" had giant relatives. Mosses such as *sphagnum moss* (2) (not related to the club mosses) grew in the ancient forests and have

climate of the tropics.

Today we can study ancient horsetails, club mosses, liverworts and giant ferns from fossils that have been preserved in rocks. We can also imagine what they were like when we see the small, living plant fossils in our woods. Next time you're walking along a stream, look around carefully. You may see a little prehistoric garden!

JOHN AND SUSAN SHAW

DINOSAURS IN TECHNICOLOR

Can you imagine a purple dinosaur as big as your house? Or one with red and yellow stripes? The fact is, we don't know what color dinosaurs really were. It's a big mystery!

Scientists study fossils to figure out what dinosaurs looked like. Most fossils are bones and teeth—the hard parts of an animal's body. Soft parts—like skin and muscles—decayed and became part of the soil.

Another kind of fossil, called a cast, was

made when a dinosaur's skin pressed against sand or mud.

But casts show only the skin's texture—bumpy, ridged or scaly. Casts don't show color!

Suppose you had never seen a zebra and you tried to imagine what one looked like by studying its bones and a cast of its skin. You could tell it was big and hairy and looked something like a horse. But you wouldn't know that it had black-and-white stripes.

Some scientists believe that dinosaurs were green, brown or gray—like the drab colors of crocodiles and Komodo dragons. But others think dinosaurs had wild, bright colors like some modern-day lizards and snakes.

Look at a reptile book and try to imagine some of those rainbow colors on a dinosaur. The emerald tree boa snake is bright green—a handsome color for a toothy *Tyrannosaurus*. The Arizona coral snake has red, white and blue stripes. Were stripes like these available in giant size for the peaceful *Brontosaurus?*

There were thousands of kinds of dinosaurs—all sizes, all shapes and probably all colors. Since we don't know what these colors were, perhaps you can paint dinosaur pictures in your imagination.

SURPRISES AROUND THE WORLD

Around the zoo
The bear must roam,
Until it sees
Its arctic home.

IT'S SPEEDY SLOTH

Faster than a speeding snail (but not much). More rapid than a burrowing worm (but not much). Able to put one foot before the other in less than a minute (sometimes). Can he be real? Can he be true?

His scientific name is *Brady-pus*, but to people who do crossword puzzles he's known as Ai—the three-toed sloth. Three? That's right. Three on each "hand" (foreleg), and three on each "foot" (hindleg). Actually the toes are more like fingers with long, curved claws.

Ai is one of the world's most relaxed creatures. He spends most of his life just hanging upside down in one Cecropia (Sih-KRO-pee-uh) tree or another. Occasionally he moves from one branch to another in search of the leaves and flowers he likes to eat. Ai's curved claws are ideal for hanging. He doesn't even have to make much of an effort to hang on. He can sleep hanging from a branch as easily as he can hang when awake. In fact, sloths have been known to remain hanging for some time after they have died.

Ai is about the size of a large, tailless cat with long legs. He has a thick body coat of long, tangled, silvery gray hair. The hair on his face is short and may be anything from white to yellow. He also has a built-in grin that makes him appear to be beaming kindly at everything in sight. However, since he is near-sighted, he probably sees little that is more than three or four feet away.

That thick mat of hair gives Ai problems. Algae and a sort of moss grow on it. So his back is a green color. This can make him hard to see among the Cecropia leaves. Also, the hair is usually infested with cockroachlike, flightless moths. They keep appearing from and disappearing into the hair as though they had a game of hide and seek going on. Having algae and moths in his hair really makes Ai smell awful.

Ai has a cousin Unau, or *Choloepus*, the two-toed sloth. This is confusing because Unau has *two* toes on his "hands," but *three* on his "feet." Unau is a bit smaller than Ai, and more common.

Both Ai and Unau are found in large numbers in jungles from the Amazon on up into Central America. They don't seem to be in any danger of becoming extinct as did an ancestor of theirs, *Megatherium*. This creature was an elephant-size ground sloth that once lived in what is now the southern part of the United States.

I doubt that Megatherium ever tried to hang upside down from tree limbs!

FRED JOHNSON

For its first few months, a young three-toed sloth (above) rides along clinging to its mother's stomach and feeding on her milk. When the baby is old enough, the mother teaches it to eat leaves and flowers. Then she sends the little sloth off to hang on its own branch.

STUCK
TOGETHER
BEAST

One day, so the story goes, Mother Nature had just about finished designing creatures. She discovered that there was quite a pile of leftover parts that didn't seem to fit anywhere. Since Mother Nature never wastes anything, she just stuck them all together.

First she chose four big, flat feet about the size of a deflated volley ball. Four high-as-a-man legs with knobby knees, which seemed ready to bend in any direction, came next. On top of the legs was a cow-and-a-half-size body covered with woolly hair that looked as though giant moth larvae had been at work on it.

At the rear of the body dangled a tired-looking, ropelike tail with a frayed end. In the middle of the back there were two great humps. (Some models had only one hump.) Up front a long curved neck led up to an ugly bony head with stiff hairy ears and big rubbery lips that didn't quite cover long, yellow front teeth. And—surprise—a pair of warm brown eyes with long handsome lashes.

It was called a camel.

In spite of their stuck-together appearance camels are among the most valuable domestic animals. People eat the meat and drink the milk. The woolly hair can be spun and woven into very fine cloth and the hide is used in many different ways. Most important of all, it can carry heavy loads for days at a time in deserts where few animals can even exist. But not without an argument!

Camels with two humps are Bactrian (BACK-tree-on), or Asian, camels. One hump camels are Arabians. One hump or two, their disposition is the same— grouchy at all times.

Camels see no reason why they should be made to work. To get a load onto one of the beasts it first has to be made to kneel down. This is done with plenty of yelling, thumping and prodding by the camel driver. The camel kicks and objects with much moaning and bellowing. Finally it flops in a heap but keeps up the complaining.

While the load is being lashed in place, the creature grumbles and keeps a sharp eye out for a chance to bite the driver or at least spit on him. Camels can spit quite accurately as far as 2.5 meters (about 8 feet).

Once the load is on, the camel stands up with a series of lurches, back end first. It still watches for a chance to bite. After a big drink of water it is ready, but usually unwilling, to join a line of other camels who have been making just as much trouble for their drivers. After more yelling and thumping, off they go at a slow gait, about

Can you imagine walking all day in the hot sun with a huge load of hay strapped to your back? That's how these camels from Afghanistan (below) spend much of their time. Camels provide cheap labor in many desert areas. Though trucks and planes have replaced the slow-moving camel in much of the Mid-East and Africa, people still use them to move goods that won't spoil on a long, hot journey.

4 kilometers (2.5 miles) an hour. They can keep this up for 12 hours at a time.

Anyone riding a camel is in for quite a trip. Camels walk the way harness racing horses pace —that is, both legs on one side move together. This makes a rolling, lurching gait that has been known to make some people "seasick." Maybe this is part of the reason why camels are called "ships of the desert."

Camels love to eat plants that other animals would never touch, and they can even drink saltwater. During the winter when it's cool and the plants they eat are extra juicy, they can survive without drinking at all. During the summer they can go about five days without a drink. After that they become very skinny and weak and may even die.

Some stories say that camels can store water in their humps or in their stomachs, but this isn't true. *Fat* is stored in the hump and used when food is very scarce. The camel's stomach is for digesting food, not for storing water.

Camels have three eyelids over each eye. Two lids have long lashes that are great for keeping out blowing sand. A third eyelid winks over the eye and wipes off any dust that may get in. Those slitlike nostrils can close up tight and also keep out sand. The camels' long, skinny necks and legs are great for getting rid of extra body heat, and camels conserve water by not sweating.

Not all camels are used to carry loads. Some are specially fed and trained for racing. These camels are called dromedaries (DROM-eh-dair-eez). Many of the rich desert sheiks have stables of racing camels as well as Arabian horses. The sheiks like to bet lots of money on camel races.

In spite of their grouchy nature some camels have been known to "fall in love" with a human. When this happens all they want to do is hang around that unfortunate person and drip green drool from their mouths on him. This happened to a famous American film star. Every time the actor appeared, one camel made great efforts to get as close to him as possible, moaning and slobbering all the while. The animal finally had to be taken out of every part of the film in which the embarrassed actor appeared.

Most camels live in Africa. Others live in Asia and Arabia. Almost all of them are domesticated. Some were once taken to Italy, Spain and northern Australia, and some of their offspring are still living there in the wild.

For centuries camel caravans (below) have been carrying great loads of carpets, grain and valuable salt through the North African desert. In ancient times it was not unusual for as many as 5,000 camels to be in a single caravan.

Most camels' coats are the same sandy brown color as the desert. But sometimes a baby (bottom) is born with white, dark brown or even black fur.

During the 1850's the United States Army brought about 80 camels to America to carry cargo from Texas to California. But the railroads were growing rapidly then, and they could carry cargo more quickly and cheaply than the camels could. The Army sold most of the camels to circuses and zoos, and some escaped to the wild. Just what became of those that escaped isn't sure, but none of them have been seen in the West for years.

Camels may look stuck-together, but they are really custom-made for surviving in the desert.

FRED JOHNSON

21

FLYING FROGS

In a tropical forest somewhere in southeastern Asia a small tree frog leaps into the air from high up in a tree. It arches its body and spreads out the wide webbing between its fingers and toes. Down it glides through the air to the limb of a tree about 35 feet away.

The flying frog leaps from branch to branch, catching some of the many flying insects that it must have for its daily food. When the frog grows tired it may just sit down on a limb and wait for the insects to fly by.

The tree frog has large, bulging eyes. They peer out well above its broad head. The frog can see in front, behind, above and to both sides all at the same time. Once in a while, though, a flying tree frog is caught off guard by a hunting tree snake or a bird.

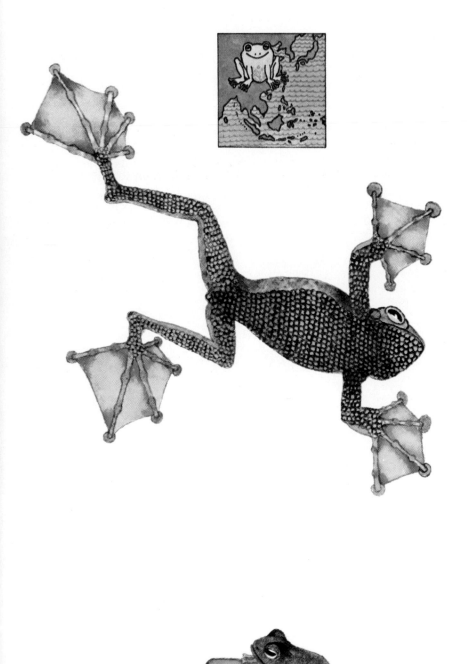

All tree frogs have large, flat discs on the tips of their toes, but flying tree frogs have discs that are huge compared to the size of their bodies. They are so big that if a frog goes gliding through the air and pushes only one toe-disc against a branch, it can hang on safely.

Little glands spread a sticky substance like glue or adhesive tape over the discs. The frog can go straight up the side of a tree or walk on the underside of a limb without falling off. It never leaves sticky footprints behind it either!

At mating time the males gather on the banks of a pond. Their calls to attract the females make the small pond a pretty noisy place. Pretty soon the females hear this loud chorus and they come leaping and gliding from the forest.

Then the frogs begin to build their nests, but not where you would think. They make them in the leaves of tree branches that hang out over the pond.

First, the female, with the male clinging tightly to her back, produces a small amount of fluid. Then she or the male, or both of them, beat this fluid with their legs until it becomes a light, foamy mass. On this bed of foam the female lays her eggs which the male fertilizes.

The female puts more fluid on top of the eggs. Again the male and female beat the fluid until it foams. Then they free themselves from the sticky mass and go leaping away among the branches, never to return.

The outside of the frothy nest soon hardens. The inner part becomes a liquid in which the tadpoles quickly hatch. After the eggs have hatched, the bottom of the nest begins to soften.

Soon the wriggling tadpoles push their way out through the nest and drop into the water below. For almost six weeks they live in the water. During that time the tadpoles lose their tails and grow legs.

One fine day they leave the water and climb into the nearest tree. Up and up they climb. They hop far out to the tip of a branch. They arch their small bodies and spread their toes. Suddenly, as though they had been doing it for years, they leap and glide down through the air on the wide, webbed soles of their new, green feet.

There are many species of flying frogs throughout southeastern Asia and down through Malaya. They are also found on the islands of Java, Sumatra and Borneo, as well as in Japan.

If you should ever happen to travel to one of these faraway places, be sure to look up. Perhaps you'll see a frog gliding through the air!

MARY MCFARLAND LEISTER

THE ADELIES OF ANTARCTICA

Imagine your mother's problems had you been born in a nest of stones, miles from any food, with temperatures below freezing and snow blowing all around. Only a penguin mother could manage under such conditions.

Adélie (uh-DAY-lee) penguins live and nest in Antarctica, one of the coldest places on earth. Seasons are upside-down in the southern hemisphere. So the handsome seabirds lay their eggs in October and November, which is summer in that part of the world. Before they can nest, however, the penguins must migrate many miles over frozen sea ice to the solid shores of Antarctica.

Adélies must have good memories. Each year they go back to the same nesting grounds, choose almost exactly the same spot, and the older birds rejoin the same mate they had the year before. Breeding colonies may number half a million on only 500 acres of ground.

Such a liking for close neighbors can have its drawbacks. The hens (females) scoop out hollows for nests and line them with stones. Then they spend hours pecking at their neighbors. Cocks (males) carry the stones to their mates and defend the nest, often getting into fights with rival males.

Two eggs are laid in the Adélie's stony nest. Then mother goes off to sea to feed, while father stays on top of the eggs for two weeks. When the hen returns from her vacation, her hungry mate leaves for his. By the time the chicks hatch, both parent birds are to-gether again and ready to care for their young.

The babies grow fast. They must, or else the terrible antarctic winter will come and bury them in snow and ice. They quickly learn to swim so they can escape one of the Adélies' main enemies, the leopard seal. They may also be in danger from predatory sea-birds, ice jams, floods, heavy surf, blizzards on shore and, of all things, overheating!

When the chicks are grown, all the Adélies leave land for winter. They spend June, July and August on the ice floes near the sea a little farther north. There the temperatures are warmer and food is more plentiful.

All during the winter-time, these funny-looking, non-flying birds will swim and play. They will eat a great deal, too. When they return to their breeding grounds in the spring they will be fat and sleek. Then they are ready to face the icy summer winds and snows that blow around their rookery.

ANNE LABASTILLE

SURPRISES BENEATH THE SEA

Help this reef fish
Find its way,
Without becoming
Someone's prey.

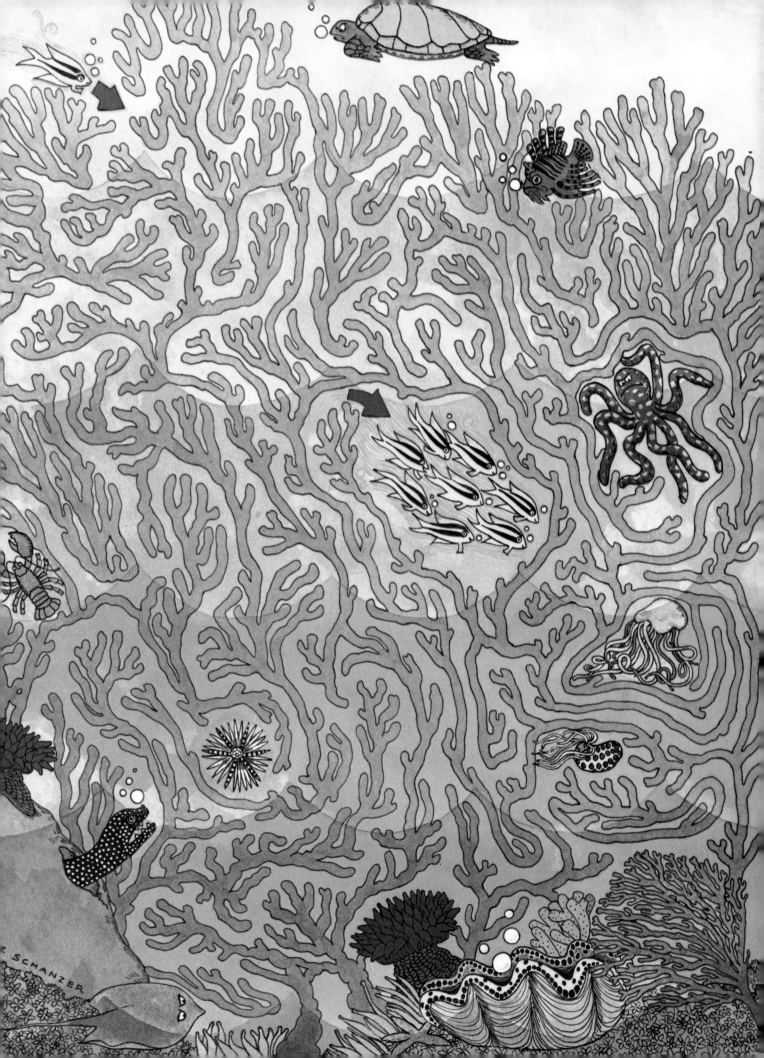

SHARKS

Ever since people first gazed upon the sea, they have been fascinated by sharks. Many stories about sharks have been told, some true, many false. How true are some of the stories you may have heard about sharks? Let's look at some of them and see.

All sharks are man-eaters. *FALSE.* Very few people are attacked by sharks each year, and only about a dozen of the over 250 different kinds of sharks are ever known to have attacked humans. Of these, the *great white shark* (below), more than any other, has earned the name "man-eater." It is the third largest shark, reaching a length of over 36 feet (11 m.). To satisfy its huge appetite, it will attack and eat almost anything, including humans.

Sharks have no enemies.
FALSE. People are the greatest predators of sharks. Besides using sharks to make fish sticks and shark-fin soup, people use them to make fertilizer, glue, leather goods and jewelry.

Killer whales may also kill sharks. And porpoises will butt sharks to death to protect themselves and their young.

Sharks lay eggs.
TRUE and FALSE. Some do. Some don't. Those that do lay eggs deposit them in a rubbery case called a mermaid's purse.

Most sharks give live birth— from 5 to 60 babies, or pups as they are called, at a time. At birth each pup is equipped with a complete set of teeth. Several rows of extra teeth lie just behind the first set. They will move up and replace those that are broken off or fall out during the shark's lifetime.

Sharks are slow moving.
FALSE. It is true that some sharks are so sluggish that you might wonder how they catch their prey. But most sharks can cruise at 5 to 10 miles (8 to 16 km.) an hour and, if the need

arises, zip through the water at up to 30 miles (48 km.) an hour. That isn't slow!

Sharks are able to smell blood in the water.
TRUE. Sharks are first drawn to noises that seem unusual. Next they rely on their keen sense of smell to find their meals. They can detect small amounts of blood from up to half a mile (0.8 km.) away.

When a shark gets near enough, its eyesight usually takes over. It may swim in circles around its prey, getting closer and closer. Or it may dart straight in to make its killing bite.

Sharks have huge appetites.
MOSTLY TRUE. Giant *whale sharks* and *basking sharks* feed on small fish and tiny animals and plants called plankton. A

few sharks gorge themselves on clams, mussels and other shelled animals. Most sharks, however, are fish-eaters. They also dine on seals, turtles, birds and almost anything else that moves.

Sometimes a group of sharks will become so excited over their meal that they work themselves into a "feeding frenzy." When this happens, they will eat anything, even logs, a boat propeller or another shark!

1

6

Sharks differ from other fish. *TRUE.* For one thing, sharks do not have skeletons made of bones as do other fish. They have tough, gristly cartilage instead—the same kind of hard, rubbery tissue you can feel at the end of your nose.

Most bony fish have flat, overlapping scales and are very slippery to hold. The scales on a shark's skin are like very tiny, hard teeth.

Most bony fish have a sac of gases called a swimbladder inside them. This keeps them from sinking. Sharks don't have swimbladders. When they stop moving they sink.

Sharks may live to an old age. *UNKNOWN.* Scientists can count the growth rings on the scales of a bony fish to tell its age, but this method doesn't work on the toothy scales of a

shark. The age of sharks is just one of the many things we still do not know about these sleek hunters of the sea.
JAMES R. NEWTON

Most sharks, like the reef whitetip (1), epaulette (2), nurse (3) and horn (4), live in shallow coastal waters. Blacktip(5) and blue sharks (6), however, are among the few that roam through the open sea.

3

2

5

4

31

THE PUFFER IS A BLUFFER

A meek, little *puffer fish* (below) swims slowly along the ocean bottom. Suddenly a small, hungry shark speeds right toward the puffer. It seems like the shark could easily swallow

Besides puffing up, some puffers have even been known to growl like a dog.

The puffer's relative, the *porcupine fish* (opposite), has spiny quills that stick straight

insides of the swallower until it is coughed up.

It can also be dangerous for humans to eat certain puffers. Some parts of them are poisonous. In Japan, however, cooked

the little fish, but the shark is in for a surprise. Before it gets too close, the clever puffer, as if by magic, changes into a big, round globe (above, right). The shark may find it hard to swallow the puffer in this shape.

The puffer is also known as the globefish, swellfish or blowfish. In deep water it swallows water, or even sand, to swell its body to as much as three times normal size. If the fish is frightened near the surface, it comes up and swallows air, puffing up like a balloon. Then it floats on its back with its big tummy sticking out above the water and tosses about on the waves like a piece of driftwood.

out when it puffs up. Woe to any fish that tries to gulp that ball of barbed wire!

The northern puffer has scaleless skin covered with close-set prickles that also stick out when it puffs up.

In spite of all these "tricks," big fish do manage to swallow an occasional puffer. But that isn't always the end of the puffer. Puffers do not have teeth, but the bones of the upper and lower jaws form cutting edges which are divided in the middle. This makes them look as though they have two big teeth above and two below. If a puffer is unlucky enough to be swallowed, it usually "chomps" on the

puffer *(fugu)* is considered a delicacy. But few cooks know how to prepare it safely. Their secret is this: On each side of a puffer is a small "fillet" of white flesh. This must be carefully removed and the rest of the fish discarded. *This* part, and *this only*, can be eaten.

A puffer may nip at your feet when you go swimming at the beach, but it will not really hurt you. Usually puffers will swell up as soon as you take them out of the water. If you catch one that doesn't, just tickle it on the tummy and it will perform its trick of blowing up into a big, round ball.

ROSALIND MANN

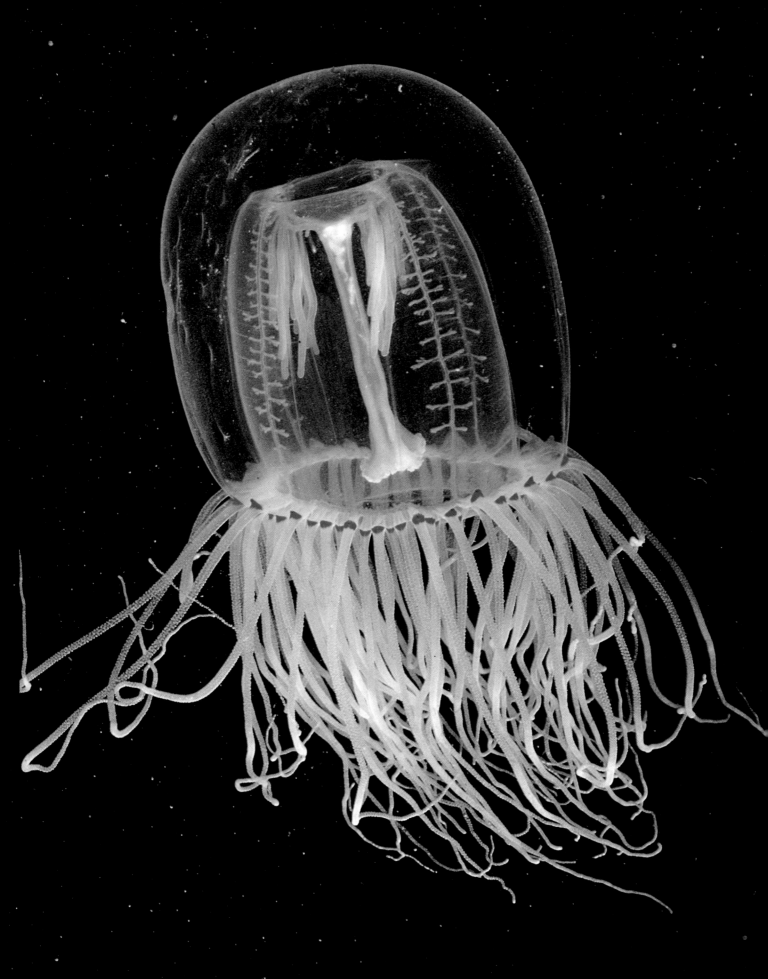

SAUCERS OF THE SEA

Imagine a "flying saucer" moving through the sea. Trailing behind you'd see a tangle of stringlike tentacles (TEN-ta-cals) and, hidden in among them, a mouth.

What a strange creature! It's a jellyfish!

Jellyfish are not fish at all. They have no skeletons as fish do. Their bodies are made up of a firm jelly, sandwiched between two layers of living cells.

These "saucers" glide through the sea by opening and closing like an umbrella, forcing water out from under them. When they stop opening and closing, they gently sink.

Most jellyfish fish for their suppers. They may glide along, waiting for a small creature to bump against a tentacle. Or they may spread their tentacles and drift down over any animals below.

The tentacles have tiny cells that contain poison. When a fish touches a tentacle, the cells shoot "darts" attached to long, hollow threads. The poison then flows through the threads and paralyzes the fish.

Perhaps you have been at a beach when a jellyfish appeared in the water. If the lifeguards made you come ashore, it was a wise thing to do. Although most jellyfish are harmless to humans, some can give you a painful sting. Even if you see a jellyfish lying on the beach, don't touch it. A tentacle can sting even if the jellyfish is dead.

There are 3,000 different kinds of jellyfish. The most common is the *moon jelly* which is found in every ocean of the world. It can be the color of a full moon or blue or pink. To eat, it collects tiny animals on its sticky tentacles. Then long "arms" around its mouth lick the food off.

Small *lion's mane jellyfish* (above) often wash up on the beaches along the Atlantic and Pacific coasts. They have flat bodies and lacy orange "arms" that net their prey. Giant cousins of the lion's mane usually live in

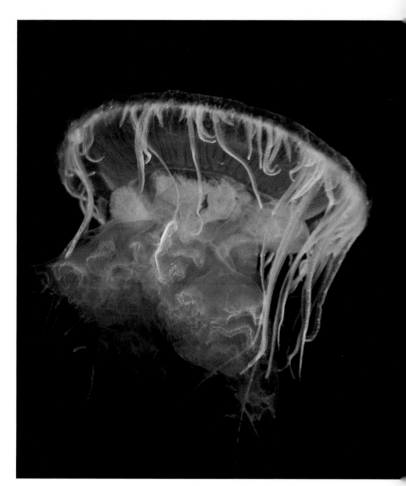

colder waters. When full-grown they can weigh as much as ten people and have as many as 800 tentacles!

If you live near one of the bays along the Pacific coast, you may have seen a *Polyorchis jellyfish* (opposite). The pink spots at the base of their tentacles are special "eyes."

They cannot really see objects, but they can sense light and dark.

Wherever you find them, jellyfish look like underwater flying saucers and umbrellas —rainbows of color with tentacles that sting. Surely they're some of the strangest creatures of all!

JANE SCHERER

SURPRISES IN TINY PLACES

This ant must
Scurry underground,
With the snack
That it has found.

IT'S THE LITTLE JUMPING SPIDER

Perhaps on a summer day you have noticed a small spider hopping about on the leaves of a shrub. If you kept watching the spider, maybe you saw it sneak up on a fly and suddenly jump, grabbing the fly with its front legs. Maybe the fly's struggling made them both topple from a leaf and fall. But instead of hitting the ground, they came to a stop in mid-air, dangling at the end of a thin silk thread. Still holding the fly, the spider climbed back up the silk thread to the leaf and settled down for a quiet meal (left). What you saw that day was one of nature's most fascinating creatures— a "jumping spider."

Not all spiders that jump are jumping spiders. Many kinds of spiders leap once in a while, especially when they are frightened. Scientists call the real jumping spiders *salticids* (SAL-tiss-ids).

You can identify them by their bright coloration, short stout bodies, short legs and the arrangement of their eyes.

They have a pair of large eyes on the front of the head. Slightly above and to the side of the large eyes is a pair of smaller eyes. On the back of the head are two other small pairs, making eight eyes altogether. Mainly because of the two large eyes in front, salticids see better than any other spiders.

Their good eyesight enables jumping spiders to spot prey from a distance and stalk it the way a cat stalks a mouse. They can see clearly up to about twenty times their own length. And they can detect things moving at even greater distances.

Another way you can recognize a jumping spider is by its uneven walk. It crawls for a few inches, stops, looks around, runs a few more inches, stops, looks around again, crouches down, and then makes a quick jump.

A jumping spider doesn't spin a web, but wherever it goes it trails a thin silk "dragline" behind it. If the spider is going to jump, it attaches the dragline firmly to the surface of a leaf so that if it misses its target and falls, it will be caught by the silk thread.

Jumping spiders also use their silk to make little cocoonlike bags (above) in which they spend the night, shed their skins, lay their eggs and protect themselves from cold weather. You can find these small "cocoons" inside rolled leaves, under rocks and in other sheltered places.

There are over 300 kinds of jumping spiders in the United States. If you have never watched one in action before, you have hours of entertainment ahead.
JAMES H. CARMICHAEL, JR.

39

WATCH OUT FOR MINI-MONSTERS!

Come explore a land of glowing mushrooms and fantastic animals! Fierce meat-eaters with crablike pincers live here. Lazy plant-eaters crawl about, nibbling on fallen leaves. Eight-eyed, hairy monsters attack strange animals that try to hop away on springs attached to their bellies. Slimy plants ooze over the ground eating everything in their paths. Where is this magical land—Africa, Australia, South America? No, it is right under your feet, under the leaves on a forest floor.

To explore this strange land you must shrink until you are smaller than a lima bean. You also must imagine the equipment you need to take—a flashlight to light the dark spaces, boots with nonslip soles to walk on the slippery leaves, and a warm sweater. Now you are ready to enter this leafy carpet of the forest floor.

First notice how many plants and animals live in this dim world. Colored *bacteria* live on the wet leaves which surround you. They take food from the leaves, helping to change them to rich black soil. Long threads of *fungi* (FUN-jie) crisscross this way and that. These, too, take food from the leaves, helping to break them down. The bacteria and the fungi together with the broken-down pieces of leaves are like the grass of a meadow—they are food for many of the plant-eaters.

As you walk along, these plant-eaters are all around you: *snails* and *worms*, *sowbugs* and *springtails*. The *sowbugs*, just a bit larger than you are, move about slowly on their seven pairs of legs. They see poorly with their small eyes. They are always moving their feelers, or antennae (an-TEN-ee), back and forth as they try to find their way around the forest floor. Sowbugs carry their young in a strange way. Just as baby pigs are found nursing at the belly of their mother (the sow), so baby sowbugs travel hidden away under the belly of the female sowbug. Good protection for such helpless babies!

Jumping, springing, hopping —what is all this motion? Insects the size of rabbits hop about everywhere. They push off the ground with tiny springs fixed to their bellies. A strange way to move about? Yes, but it helps these *springtails* escape the predators that hide everywhere. For the forest floor is a scene of chases, fights and sudden death. You, too, must be careful to keep away from these fearsome meat-eaters.

What is that *clack-clack-clacking* around the fallen twig to your right? It grows louder! You had better hide behind a piece of twig until it passes. A crablike creature the size of a beagle dog stalks toward you. It clicks its two pincers as it moves forward. Has it spotted you? No, it notices a springtail nearby and grabs it with one claw. You hear the crunching sound as the springtail becomes food for the *pseudo-scorpion* (SOOD-o-scorp-eon), or "false scorpion." The pseudo-scorpion is well named. With its pincers and jointed body, it looks like the scorpions that live in the deserts of the Southwest.

You hear another loud noise, the sound of heavy footsteps. What beast now approaches? A

R. S.

hairy, brown spider as big as a bear walks forward. Its eight sharp eyes have spotted the pseudoscorpion. With its two fangs ready, it plans to paralyze the pseudoscorpion and drain the juices from its body. But the pseudoscorpion turns and runs into a narrow space between two leaves. The spider waits, tries to follow, then gives up and begins to walk away. This is a *wolf spider*, a large female. From the rear you can see her 30 babies clinging tightly to her back, a safe place in this battleground under the carpet of leaves.

Another animal, as long as a school bus, comes close. Will it try to eat you? No, this is a *millipede* nibbling on dead leaves, moving slowly this way and that, its hundreds of legs in motion. With its poor sight and hearing, it is protected from predators by its thick plates of armor, its large size and a strong odor it gives off. You watch it crawl away, then you walk on to discover the other animals living in this strange land.

Careful! Careful where you walk! Look down and see that sticky blob at your feet. It moves! But so slowly. See how it flows over and swallows the bacteria. This queer mass of jelly appears to be neither plant nor animal. It moves like an amoeba (a-MEE-buh), oozing

along. Yet it reproduces by tiny, seedlike spores, as do some plants. This *slime mold* is nothing more than naked living matter that dwells in wet places wherever there are decaying leaves, twigs and branches.

What huge animal now appears from around the stick ahead? Nearly as large as the millipede, it moves forward on many legs. Nervously it looks around and darts forward. This is no plant-eater! It sees too well and moves too fast! This *centipede* has spotted you and runs toward you, its poisonous fangs waving. Quickly you must make yourself bigger if you are going to escape!

Hurry! Grow! Change back to your real size! Quick. . . !

Now the tiny centipede runs harmlessly across your boot. You have survived your fantastic journey to the forest floor.

RICHARD FIDLER

THE AMAZING ANT

I could lift 23 cars over my head at one time. Or I could enter the Olympics and lift weights weighing over 67,000 pounds for an unbeatable world record. Yes, I could . . . if I had the strength of an ant. And I would weigh only 150 pounds!

Ants are one of the strongest insects. An ant may lift more than 450 times its weight. It can carry a dead moth or a caterpillar or some other insect much larger than itself.

Ants are close relatives of wasps, hornets and bees. There are about 14,000 kinds of ants in the world.

They eat almost everything —candy bars, berries, tree sap, caterpillars . . . and picnic lunches. And ants can live almost anywhere. They build their nests in the walls of houses, beneath rocks, inside logs and in the ground.

More amazing than these facts is the orderly way in which ants live. Like many of their bee and wasp relatives, ants live in a large, well-organized group called a colony.

A colony may contain as few as a dozen ants to over a million. There are three types of ants in every colony—and each has its own job.

The *queen* has only one duty. She spends her whole life laying eggs for the colony. She may live for as long as 15 to 20 years.

During that time she is totally waited on by the *workers*.

Most of the ants in the colony are workers. They are females that never develop fully. They don't grow wings and usually are smaller and cannot have offspring. Their job is to care for the queen and her offspring and to fight off enemies. They also build, repair and clean the nest. The workers' biggest job is to make sure the colony is well fed.

Many ant species get their food from aphids. Aphids feed on plant juices and give off a honeydew liquid that the ants eat. By stroking an aphid's abdomen with their antennae, the ants cause the aphid to produce more honeydew drops than it normally would. This is called milking the aphids.

At a special time of the year the *males* are formed. Their only job is to mate with new queens that are formed at the same time.

Both the young queens and the males have wings. On a late summer afternoon their mating flight begins. The queens and males take to the air together and form a large swarm. They mate in the air and the males die shortly afterward.

Then the young queens bite or rub off their wings and start looking for a sheltered place to begin a new colony.
STEPHEN J. KRASEMANN

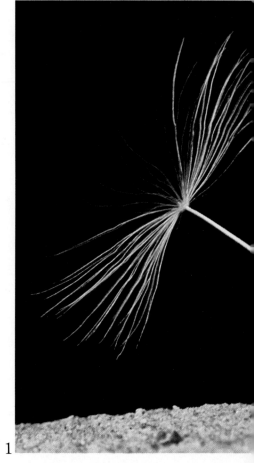

1

3

44

Ants have many unusual ways of making a living.

Harvester ants (1) gather seeds during the growing season and store them underground. In spring and winter, when no food can be found, they chew the seeds up and make "ant bread."

Leaf cutter ants (2) snip off pieces of leaves and pile them up in big underground "rooms." A fungus grows on the leaves, and this is what the ants eat.

Many other ants live off the honeydew produced by aphids (3). These ants, in turn, guard the aphids from predators.

Honey ants (4) have another strange life style. Some of the young ants act as storage tanks for the sweet liquids gathered by the workers.

Tailor ants (5) are talented seamstresses. They sew leaves into nests to protect themselves from bad weather and enemies.

2

4

5

BUTTERFLY MAGIC

Butterflies have four stages in their lives—egg, larva (caterpillar), pupa (chrysalis) and adult. At each stage, they almost magically turn into something totally different.

The *gulf fritillary*, like all butterflies, begins life as a pale, tiny egg (1). Within a few days, a caterpillar hatches by eating its way out of the egg. Once free, the caterpillar eats so much that it outgrows its skin several times (2, a newly hatched and a full-grown caterpillar).

When the caterpillar is large enough, it attaches itself to a stem (3), sheds its skin once more, and becomes a chrysalis (KRIS-uh-lis) (4). The chrysalis can't move, but inside its shell big changes are taking place (5).

The butterfly that crawls from the chrysalis (6) looks nothing like the caterpillar. It has wet, crumpled wings that it pumps full of liquid. When the wings dry (7), it flies off to find a mate and begin the cycle again.

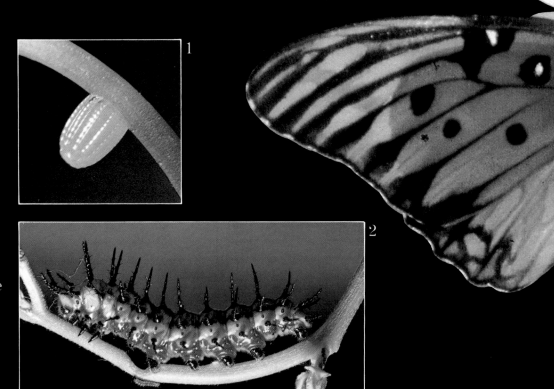

7

5

SURPRISES
IN BIG SIZES

These elephants
Will take a stroll,
Until they find
The waterhole.

BIG BIRD

Remember the old story about how the ostrich sticks its head in the sand so enemies won't see it? As you probably know, that story isn't true. But how did such a silly story get started?

Perhaps some explorer long ago saw an ostrich sitting on a nest. As the explorer crept closer, the ostrich suddenly lowered its long neck and stretched it flat—just a few inches above the sand.

This probably looked like very strange behavior to the explorer. But today we know the ostrich was using a survival trick to help hide from predators! When an ostrich stretches out its neck and lies very still, the whole bird seems to disappear. It suddenly looks like a big bush or a mound of earth!

We don't need to make up silly stories about ostriches— they're unusual enough as it is! They are, for example, the largest birds in the world. When a full-grown male, or *cock*, ostrich stands up and looks

An ostrich family takes off across the African plains in search of food (below).

The babies, who are only a month old, can move just as fast as their parents. But they still need help escaping from predators. When Mom and Dad are nearby, most animals are afraid to bother the chicks. *Even when they are left alone, the babies aren't completely defenseless. For their first few months, both males and females have feathers the same color as dried grass so predators don't always see them.*

around, his head may tower as much as 2½ meters (about 8 feet) above the ground. The female, or *hen*, is slightly smaller. An ostrich's head is a little bigger than a canta- loupe, but flat on the top and bottom. Its eyes are as large as tennis balls. And it has long lashes on the upper lids that help keep blowing sand out of its eyes.

The ostrich's long, down-covered neck looks something like a fat snake. Its long, nearly naked legs look like huge Thanksgiving turkey drumsticks. Its stubby wings are use- less for flying. But the wings have beautiful, extra-large feathers called plumes on the ends. The ostrich uses these fancy feathers to show off to other os- triches and to shelter its grapefruit-size eggs from the sun.

This gawky, awk- ward-looking bird is really quite graceful. It can jog along with great, springy steps of about 4 meters (13 feet), and can run up to 65 kilometers (about 40

51

After six weeks of nesting, a pair of proud ostriches stand back and watch their babies hatch (opposite).

The chicks inside the eggs kick and struggle and tap hard with their beaks to make the first, small holes in their shells. After more pecking, one of the chicks manages to crack its shell all the way around one end. When the egg finally breaks open (below), an ostrich as big as a full-grown chicken struggles out (bottom).

As soon as it dries, the newborn will be on its feet looking for something to eat.

miles) an hour to escape from predators such as lions. When several ostriches are running, their feathers and plumes wave and flutter in the breeze and make a very pretty sight.

What kind of voice does the ostrich have? If you could cross a lion with a large snake, you might get a sound close to it. Ostriches have a strange, deep roar mixed with a loud hissing sound.

Ostriches are usually seen on the dry, sandy plains of East Africa, in the company of antelopes, zebras and other grazing animals. Early explorers probably thought this was a very strange animal "family." But there is a good reason why these animals live together. Ostriches and grazing animals help each other. The ostrich, with its head held high in the air and its keen eyesight, makes a good "lookout" for danger. In return, the other animals stir up mice, birds, lizards and insects as they graze. These make a tasty

addition to the seeds and plants that the ostrich usually eats.

Ostriches used to roam over western Asia and large areas of Africa, but they disappeared mainly because humans killed too many for their beautiful plumes. Luckily, before the ostriches were all killed it was discovered that they would live and breed in captivity. Ostrich farms were started in many parts of the world to supply people with plumes to decorate hats. The plumes were plucked twice a year from the males with no harm to the birds.

Ostriches in captivity do something that they seldom do in the "wild." They gobble up shiny objects! Bottle caps, bits of glass, aluminum foil—anything shiny or glittery is an attractive tidbit to an ostrich. One ostrich even swallowed a small alarm clock! Wouldn't it have been funny to have seen that alarm clock going down that long neck? *Tick! Gulp! Tick! Gulp!*

FRED JOHNSON

HOW BIG IS BIG?

Have you ever wondered just how big the biggest animals really are? Do you know which ones are the tallest, the longest and the heaviest?

A group of these giant birds, mammals, reptiles and amphibians is gathered below. Take a look at these animals and then read all about them.

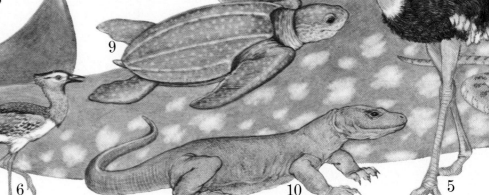

1 The biggest mammal is the *blue whale*. A blue whale can be 100 feet long and can weigh almost 200 tons. (That means it's as long as three school buses parked end to end, and weighs as much as 30 elephants!) Blue whales are in extreme danger of becoming extinct because people have overhunted them.

2 The biggest *land* mammal is the *African elephant*. An average male is about 10 feet tall (measuring from its toes to the top of its shoulders) and weighs about 6 tons. The biggest elephant ever reported was over 13 feet tall and weighed 12 tons. (That's about how much *13* Volkswagon Beetles weigh!)

3 The *whale shark*, biggest of the fish, weighs up to 45 tons and measures 50 feet or more in length. Its babies hatch from 12-inch-long eggs that are the largest laid by any living animal. Fortunately for human swimmers, this rare shark is peaceful and only eats small animals and plants called plankton. The whale shark can be found in the warm waters of the Atlantic, Pacific and Indian Oceans.

4 The bird with the longest wingspan is the *wandering albatross.* Its wings can measure 11 feet from tip to tip. The albatross spends most of its life at sea south of the equator. It uses its great wings to soar and glide above the water as it searches for food. To satisfy an appetite as huge as its size, the albatross must eat almost continuously. Its favorite foods are fish, squid and crustaceans which live near the surface of the ocean. It will even eat trash thrown overboard from ships.

5 The world's biggest non-flying bird is the *North African ostrich*. An adult male stands 8 feet tall and weighs up to 345 pounds. Even though the bird can't fly, it can run faster than 30 miles an hour without seeming tired. The ostrich also lays the largest eggs of any living bird. An average-size one weighs about 3½ pounds. And they are so thick and tough that it would take the blow of a hammer to crush one.

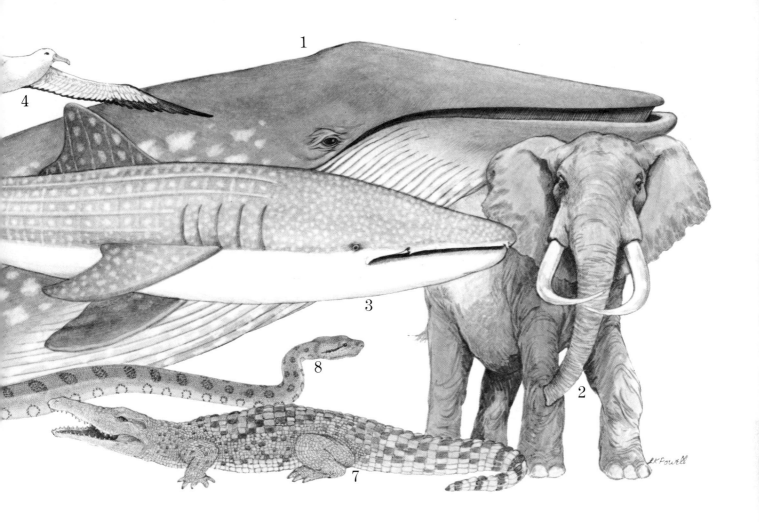

6 The heaviest flying bird is the *kori bustard*, a long-beaked bird found in East and South Africa. The male, or cock, can weigh 40 pounds. If the bird were much heavier, it wouldn't be able to fly at all. As it is, kori bustards only take to the air for short distances when they are in danger.

7 The biggest reptile, the *saltwater crocodile*, lives in waters off Southeast Asia and northern Australia. Adult males usually weigh about 1,000 pounds and are about 15 feet long. But the biggest male ever recorded measured 28 feet from end to end—nearly twice the average size. These giants have a reputation as the fiercest man-eaters on earth.

8 The biggest snakes in the world are the *anaconda* of South America and the *reticulated* (reh-TICK-u-lay-ted) *python*, which lives in Southeast Asia. The anaconda takes the prize for being the heaviest and the reticulated python, which averages 25 feet in length, is the longest. Both snakes are constrictors that kill by squeezing their victims so tightly that they die of suffocation.

9 The world's biggest turtle is the giant *leatherback sea turtle*. It is 6 to 7 feet long and weighs up to 1,000 pounds. Most of this turtle's life is spent at sea but it comes ashore to lay its eggs.

10 The biggest lizard is the *Komodo dragon*. It grows to 10 feet and can weigh 300 pounds. Komodo dragons eat young deer and wild pigs. However, when they bite one, it may not die right away. An infection from the Komodo's saliva usually kills the victim.

11 The rare *Goliath frog* of West Africa is the biggest frog in the world. One giant, the first Goliath frog ever captured, had a 10-inch-long body. Another specimen weighed almost 7½ pounds and measured 32 inches from its nose to the end of its extended rear legs. And supposedly an even bigger one got away!

ROBERT GRAY

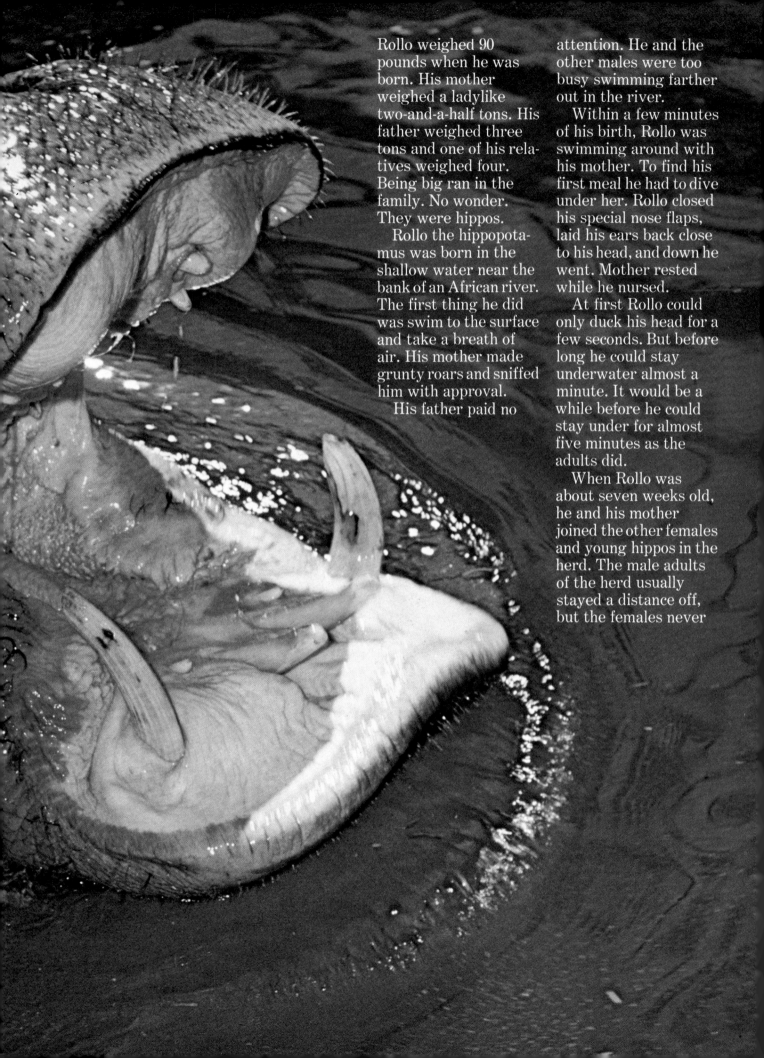

Rollo weighed 90 pounds when he was born. His mother weighed a ladylike two-and-a-half tons. His father weighed three tons and one of his relatives weighed four. Being big ran in the family. No wonder. They were hippos.

Rollo the hippopotamus was born in the shallow water near the bank of an African river. The first thing he did was swim to the surface and take a breath of air. His mother made grunty roars and sniffed him with approval.

His father paid no attention. He and the other males were too busy swimming farther out in the river.

Within a few minutes of his birth, Rollo was swimming around with his mother. To find his first meal he had to dive under her. Rollo closed his special nose flaps, laid his ears back close to his head, and down he went. Mother rested while he nursed.

At first Rollo could only duck his head for a few seconds. But before long he could stay underwater almost a minute. It would be a while before he could stay under for almost five minutes as the adults did.

When Rollo was about seven weeks old, he and his mother joined the other females and young hippos in the herd. The male adults of the herd usually stayed a distance off, but the females never

Mom watches for danger as Rollo snuggles close (below). If he tries to go exploring on his own, she'll give him a good, hard shove that knocks him off his feet.

Rollo's father is busy swimming in a nearby river. When he's ready for a snooze, he rests his head on the back of a friend (bottom).

In a year Rollo was a fat one of 700 pounds (below)! Now he could doze by the river and not worry much about crocodiles. After two years Rollo weighed 1,500 pounds and his mother chased him from the nursery. It was time for him to join the other males on the edge of the herd.

got too far from the young. If Rollo's mother left for a short while, the other females would act as "aunts" and take care of him.

It was a good thing that the hippo "aunts" helped watch the nursery. Hungry crocodiles and lions often came to find a meal in the shallow water near the bank. The young hippos would be easy prey, but no predator dared challenge the huge adults.

Sometimes the herd gathered on the bank or on a sandbar in the river to roll in the mud and sunbathe. They would wallow about and take snoozes. When Rollo needed a rest, he clambered up onto his mother's back or any nearby female's and fell fast asleep.

Despite their huge bodies, hippos have tender skin. Ticks and biting insects are always bothering them. Egrets, oxpeckers and other birds land on their backs and walk about, eating the pests.

The hippos like this. But the hot, African sun is another problem. If

the hippos get too dry, their skin could burn and crack. Hippos have no sun-tan lotion to help them. But they do have something just as good: They can "sweat" a pink, oily fluid that keeps their skin moist.

At night Rollo's herd led quite another life. In the cool darkness they came ashore and often wandered many miles from the river, eating all the way.

After the hippos had passed through, the ground looked as though bulldozers had been working it over. Local natives raising crops would find them leveled. Once Rollo's herd grazed an entire truck garden and then stripped the bushes around a poor farmer's property. Rollo tagged along with the herd, doing his best to keep up with the eating.

Rollo grew up quickly. By the time he was two years old, he was big enough to go live with the other adult males. At first, he didn't want to leave his mother so he kept trying to come back and

join the females. They had to chase him away over and over again. By this time his mother had another baby. She was far too busy to be bothered with Rollo.

Soon Rollo didn't mind being on his own. He ate and swam and rolled in the mud with all the other fat ones.
FRED JOHNSON

SURPRISES IN DISGUISES

Dressed in white
To match the snow,
This lemming sneaks
Past every foe.

THE SECRET WORLD OF THE OCTOPUS

All day long Onta the octopus huddles in her cave. She is afraid to be seen by anything that lives beneath the waves—even another octopus. So she hides in this secret place until it is night and there are shadows in the sea. Then most of the ocean feels like her cave, dark and safe, and she comes out in search of food.

Squeezed almost flat, Onta's boneless body flows through the narrow opening in the rocks.

Gently she drops onto the ocean bottom. She pulls herself forward from place to place, using the suckers on her eight rubbery limbs to clutch the ground in front of her. As she walks, her body is constantly changing color so that it blends with her surroundings. Now she is as pink (left) as a branch of coral just ahead, but with one more step she becomes tan (below) because of a nearby rock.

Deep in a cave, Onta keeps watch over her fragile clusters of eggs. She gently cradles them in her arms (below), never resting until the babies are born. Her suckers are used like tiny vacuum cleaners to remove any dirt that may have landed on the eggs. This constant activity and the jets of water that Onta shoots at the clusters keep the water in the cave churned up so the eggs stay fresh and clean.

These rainbow colors help Onta fool the small, toothed whales and moray eels that are her worst enemies. But in case they do see through her colorful disguises, there is another trick she can play on them. Panicked by an approaching eel, Onta squirts a puff of black ink into the water, then turns a ghostly white and jets away. She is lucky this time—her attacker heads for the murky cloud instead of for her. She escapes.

While she retreats, Onta swims backward and looks to see if she is being followed by the eel. When she sees that she is no longer in any danger, Onta lands again on the sea floor and resumes her hunting.

Now the hungry octopus slides the feathery tips of her arms into every hole she passes. She is hoping to catch a crab or a lobster for her dinner. Later she may crouch behind some rocks and try to ambush a small crab that scuttles by.

After she has eaten, Onta perches on a mound close to her cave. The colors glowing in her body show that she is satisfied and at peace. But this pleasant feeling doesn't last very long. There is a shadow, a movement, a sudden swiftness in the water that alarms her, ending her moment of rest.

Expecting a fight, Onta raises her arms. Like lassos about to be

tossed, they twist in tiny circles around her head. But tonight she will not be challenged. This intruder is a male octopus who has come to court her, not to fight. Onta is being told this by the signals that the stranger is making with his body. Because he is colored in brilliant stripes, she is sure that he does not want to harm her. There is no anger in either of them as they touch. The male gently places one of

his arms into an opening in Onta's body. Small packages of sperm flow from his body, along a groove in his arm and into Onta. Then the mating is over.

It is many weeks before the ivory-colored eggs that contain her babies appear. They come out of her attached to slender stalks, like beads on a string. As each of the strands flows out, Onta hangs it from the roof of her cave. She has spawned

When the tiny octopi are ready
to be born, Onta cannot do anything to help them. They must
struggle from their egg cases
(below) alone. As each baby
pushes against the opening of its
egg, dozens of colors flash in
its body. The harder it strains,
the more it sparkles and glows.
Finally its back end breaks
through. Then its head and arms
wriggle out and it is born into
the sea (bottom).

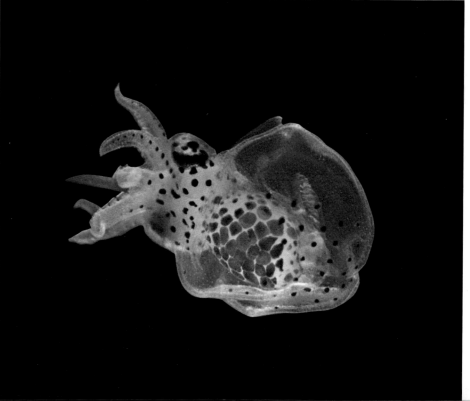

thousands of eggs, and all she
thinks about now is caring for
them until they begin to hatch.
    When the tiny octopi finally
struggle from their egg cases
and swim out of the cave, Onta
is close to death. Caring for the
eggs has left her too weak to
move. She may not recover, but
her babies will take her place
in the sea.

DR. GEORGE D. RUGGIERI, S.J.
AND NORMAN DAVID ROSENBERG

ACTING FIERCE

What a surprise a bird gets when it tries to capture a tasty-looking *praying mantis!* Suddenly the mantis (below) rears up, spreads its wings, and looks very fierce—so fierce, in fact, that the bird usually flies on in search of easier prey.

But the mantis is only pretending to be dangerous. Some animals act much fiercer than they really are to protect themselves from predators.

Nature gives every animal a "bag of tricks" to help it fool its enemies. Insects like the praying mantis match the colors of their surroundings so hungry birds won't spot them. If that doesn't work, then the mantis may resort to a final trick and try frightening enemies away.

A *spicebush swallowtail caterpillar* (opposite, top) puts on a different type of fierce act. Those huge, scary

eyes on its back are just spots of color. But if the caterpillar is lucky, a hungry bird will think the spots are the eyes of a snake. And most birds won't tangle with a snake.

An *Io moth* (below) may look like an easy meal to a bird. But when the bird touches one with its bill, the moth flashes a pair of big, fake eyes. For an instant, the bird thinks it is face to face with an owl. That moment of fear is all the time the moth needs to escape.

FOUR DISAPPEARING ACTS

There are four animals hidden on these pages. Can you find them? Cover up the answers and try to trace the outline of each creature with your finger.

Each animal seems to disappear because its color and shape match its surroundings. That's how an animal remains

1

2

in plain view without predators and prey recognizing it as a hungry enemy or a tasty meal.

Looking like a rock or part of a plant is one great way of "disappearing." *Spotted scorpion fish* (1) use this trick to get food without working at it. Resting on the ocean bottom, they look like moss-covered rocks, not fish. So smaller fish aren't afraid to swim near them. When the prey get close enough the scorpion fish gobbles them up.

Walking sticks (2) pose as parts of plants to keep from being eaten. It's almost impossible for a predator to see their long, skinny bodies among tall blades of grass.

Another way animals hide is by matching the colors and patterns of their surroundings. *Ptarmigan* (3) change color with the seasons.

In summer their feathers are brown to blend with the rocks around them. White feathers replace the brown ones in winter.

Some *moths* (4) hide by landing on a lichen that is the same color as their wings. Then if they hold very still, they become almost invisible.

3

4

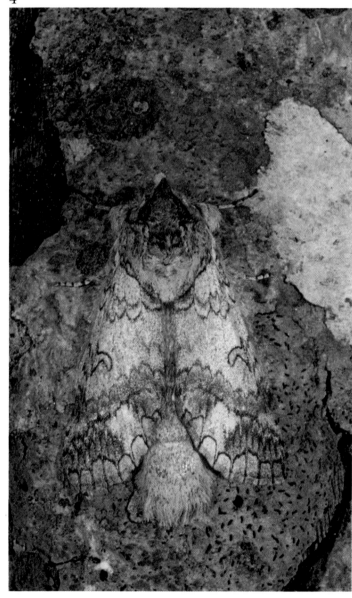

69

SURPRISES FROM HEAD TO TAIL

From head to tail
The tick must go.
The birds will eat it
If it's slow.

TALE OF TAILS

Did you know that when you were about one month old you had a tail? Not one month after you were born, but one month after you began to grow inside your mother's body. By the time you were born, your tail was gone and you never even missed it.

Some animals would have trouble if they lost their tails. Some need tails to swim and some to fly, some to swing and some to build. And some need tails to say to a female, "I'm handsome, and if you stay with me we can raise a family."

That is what a *male turkey* (opposite) is saying when he spreads out his tail feathers like a fan. This fancy tail also helps the bird fly, which is what birds' tails mostly do.

One of the noisiest tails you will ever come across belongs to the *rattlesnake* (right). A rattlesnake isn't born with its rattles —it grows them. When it is born it has a button at the end of its tail. As the snake grows it sheds its skin. Each time the skin is shed another ring is uncovered at the base of its tail. Air dries the ring and when the snake shakes its tail, the rings rattle against one another.

Tails do many wonderful things. If you still had a tail, what do you suppose you would use it for?

NATALIE S. RIFKIN

A kangaroo (above) uses its tail and legs as a kind of three-legged stool. The tail also helps the kangaroo keep its balance as it bounds across Australia's woodlands and plains with 20- to 40-foot jumps. What fun that must be for the little kangaroo riding in its mother's pouch.

73

TRICKY TONGUES

1

2

Stand in front of a mirror. Open your mouth wide and say "ah-h." What do you see? Your pink, flat tongue.

Your tongue is very important to you. It helps you chew and swallow your food. (Pay attention to how your tongue moves next time you eat.) It tells you whether your food is sweet or sour, salty or bitter, hot or cold. And for you, a human being, it has an even more important job—it helps you talk!

Other animals need their tongues as much as you do, even though they don't speak. Some animals wouldn't be able to eat if it weren't for their tongues, because their tongues are their most important tool for getting food. And they use their tongues to "handle" food as they chew and swallow.

Giraffes (1) have long, flexible tongues and a prehensile upper insects. Their tongues can reach a distance as long as their body and tail, and even longer!

Spying an insect with its bulging eyes, a chameleon slowly moves into striking range. In a flash—faster than your eye can see—the chameleon zips out its tongue, snares the prey with the sticky tip, and pulls it back into its mouth.

Most *frogs* (3) and *toads* are members of this shooting tongue

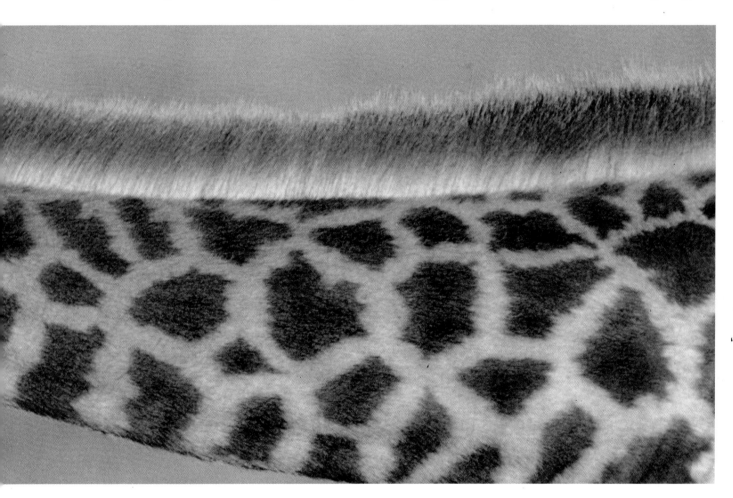

lip that they curl around leaves and use to pull the leaves from trees. These two features work so well together that giraffes can munch leaves from the thorniest acacia tree without feeling any consequences.

Most animals' tongues are attached at the back of the mouth. But *chameleons'* (2) tongues are attached at the front so they can shoot them forward to catch unsuspecting parade, too. They flip their tongues out at any small, wiggling target that moves too close. When a victim is safely captured, the toad or frog lifts its head and closes its eyes. The eyes sink down and help push the food down its throat.

The *anteater* (4) would never be able to satisfy its giant appetite for ants and termites by picking them up one at a time. It has to get food in king-size amounts—and its tongue helps it do this quickly and easily.

An anteater may search for ant and termite nests hour after hour. When it finds one, it tears the nest apart. Then it jabs into the nest with its 60-centimeter-long (2 feet) tongue and the insects stick by the hundreds!

Members of the *woodpecker* (5) family capture prey with different types of slender, hard-tipped tongues. One common type of tongue is lance-shaped. Woodpeckers use it to spear a favorite kind of food—large insects. First the woodpecker uses its chisellike bill to find an insect's tunnel in a tree. Then out comes the long tongue, feeling along the tunnel until ZAP! it stabs its prey.

Geckos (6), a kind of lizard, usually use their tongues for catching insects. But when the see-through coverings over their

3

5

4

6

eyes get dirty, the geckos can flip up their tongues and wipe the coverings clean.

If you have ever been licked by a *cat* you certainly noticed how rough its tongue felt. The center of a cat's tongue is covered with short, fat, pointed bumps. These bumps help wild cats, such as *leopards* (7), lick meat off the bones of prey. They also work like the teeth of a comb when cats clean themselves.

Domestic cats need their tongues for another very important job: letting you know how much they like you!

Not every animal's tongue may be as exciting as a chameleon's or as friendly as a cat's, but it does the job it has to do. Next time you see a tongue in action, take a really close look at it. Is it licking, sticking, grabbing or stabbing?

SHIRLEY MEEKER

THE UNICORN WAS A NARWHAL

Long ago, in the Middle Ages, people believed in unicorns. They thought the unicorn looked like a large deer with one long, twisted, ivory horn growing from its forehead.

The trouble was nobody had ever *seen* a unicorn. People only heard rumors about it from explorers. But they thought the animal must live on earth, since they had seen its horn.

Unicorn horns were very valuable. Each one was worth many times its weight in gold. The reason for this was the belief that the horn had the power to make poison harmless. So emperors and kings, who worried that someone might poison them, were only too glad to pay royally for drinking cups made from the wonderful horn.

Today we know that no such animal as the unicorn ever existed. But where did those long horns come from? They came from whales!

These whales are called narwhals (NAR-walls), and they live only in the arctic seas near the North Pole. They are rare animals. Scientists say there are only about 20,000 narwhals in the world.

Narwhals are small members of the whale family. They grow to be 4 to 5 meters (about 16 feet) long. A narwhal baby, which is called a calf, is 1.5 meters long. When it is born, it is dark slate blue. Adults are lighter colored with dark brown backs, lightly spotted sides and grayish white bellies.

Only the male grows a horn, which is really a giant, overgrown, left front tooth. It grows straight out through the narwhal's upper lip. It is twisted like a corkscrew, and can be 3 meters long. This tooth (or *tusk*, as it is usually called) is hollow. The hollow center is filled with spongy pulp and nerves, just like your teeth. Occasionally someone sees a narwhal with a broken tusk with the end open and inflamed. He may be suffering from a giant-size toothache!

What does the male narwhal do with his beautiful tusk? There are many theories. Do they use their tusks like swords to fight each other? Do they use them to poke holes in the polar ice? Probably not, because the tusks could break off if they're used as swords or giant icepicks.

Another theory is that narwhals use their tusks to spear cuttlefish, squid and crustaceans—which they like to eat. If this is true, then catching food would be difficult for the females, who have no tusks.

The most widely accepted theory is that a male uses his tusk in courtship display. But no one has been able to solve this mystery for sure.

FRED BRUEMMER

WHO'S LOOKING AT YOU?

Can you name the animals staring at you from these pages? Each of them has eyes that will tell you something about its lifestyle. Before you read the answers (printed upside down below), here are a few hints.

Predators often have eyes close together on the front of the face. This helps them focus both eyes on their prey. Monkeys and other primates have

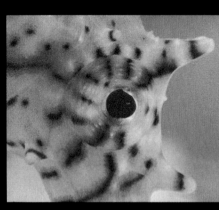
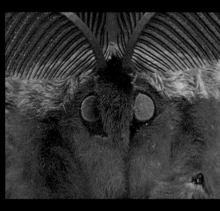

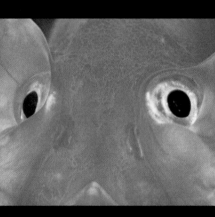
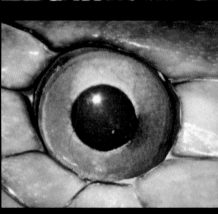

Top: coyote
Middle: tiger
Bottom: bald eagle

Top: sea horse
Middle: three-horned chameleon
Bottom: goldfish

Top: Polyphemus moth
Middle: rainbow lorikeet (bird)
Bottom: king cobra

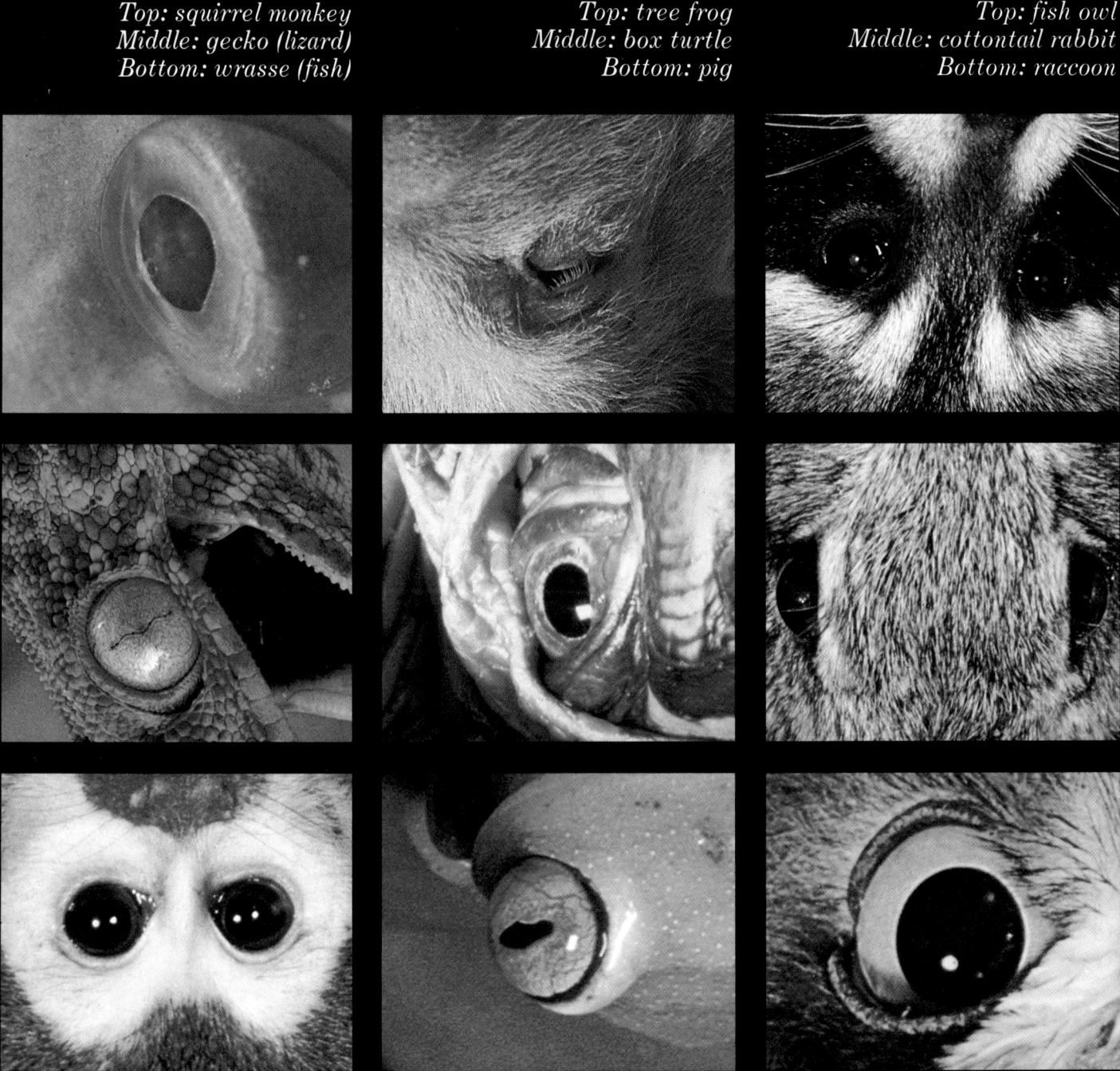

Top: squirrel monkey
Middle: gecko (lizard)
Bottom: wrasse (fish)

Top: tree frog
Middle: box turtle
Bottom: pig

Top: fish owl
Middle: cottontail rabbit
Bottom: raccoon

SURPRISES FOR A STORMY NIGHT

Find the house,
Don't lose the trail.
The spooks will get you
If you fail.

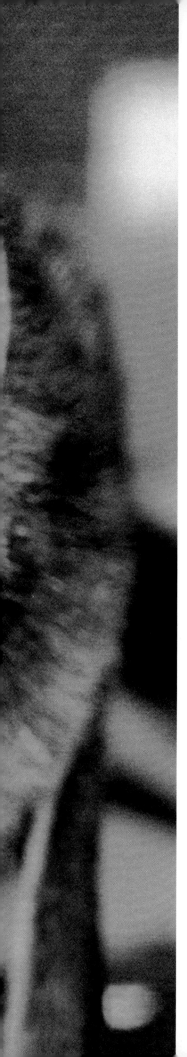

BATS

When you think of black magic, ghosts and witches, do you also think of bats? Lots of people do! Maybe this is because many bats live in dark caves and are active at night. And when some people think of darkness and bats, they think of spooky things.

This bad reputation is very unfair to bats. Most bats are harmless and none can cast an evil spell! But bats continue to be feared because most people really know little about them.

How many bats live on earth?
Billions and billions and billions! There are more bats than any other mammal—except rodents. And they live almost everywhere. Scientists have found about 850 kinds of bats in all parts of the world except in the Antarctic, the Arctic tundra and on a few oceanic islands.

What do bats eat?
Almost all North American bats dine on insects. However, there are fruit bats that eat fruit, flowers and nectar. Some bats feast on blood. Other bats eat fish, small mammals and birds.

Can bats really fly?
Bats are the only mammals that

A vampire bat shows off teeth so sharp that its victims don't even wake up when bitten.

can fly. (Mammals such as flying squirrels are misnamed. They don't fly at all—they just *glide* through the air.)

A bat's wings are thin, leathery, elastic pieces of skin. You can get an idea of what this skin is like by spreading the thumb and first finger of your hand. The double layer of skin that you have stretched thin is a little like a bat's wing—only the bat's wing is much bigger and stretches from all its fingers to its body, back and tail!

Are bats blind?
No, the expression "blind as a bat" is false. All bats have good eyesight, but most don't use their eyes to hunt or fly at night. Bats fly by *echolocation*. They use echoes to find food and to avoid flying into obstacles in the dark. In a sense, bats "see" with their ears.

While flying, a bat sends out short, high squeaks from its mouth or nose. These sounds bounce off objects and echo back to the bat's ears. Acting like a computer, the bat's brain uses the echoes to figure out the size and movements of an object and how far away it is.

Do bats fly into your hair?
No, that age-old belief is untrue. However, a bat may fly close to your head and that may frighten you!

A little brown bat (left) will catch and eat a meal of insects while in flight. Hanging upside down, a tube-nosed fruit bat (opposite) dines more restfully.

Although most bats won't hurt you, *don't handle them.* Like most wild animals, a bat can become frightened if it is trapped or handled—and it may bite. Bats may have rabies, a disease that you can catch if you're bitten by a rabid bat.

What do bats do during the day? Tropical fruit bats sleep in trees during the day, hanging by their toes. Most North American bats roost in dark places —rocky crevices, hollow trees or attics. Caves are favorite roosts for large colonies, especially in winter when many bats are hibernating. In the Southwest, some bats use limestone caves as summer nurseries for thousands and thousands of baby bats! For example, Bracken Cave in Texas houses an estimated *twenty million bats!* When they fly from the cave at twilight they cover the sky like a giant cloud of smoke.

Why do I like bats? They're such interesting creatures! Who wouldn't be fascinated by a small mammal that flies with its hands, "sees" with its ears, and sleeps hanging by its toes?
SIGMUND A. LAVINE

To hibernate, endangered Indiana bats (right) crowd so closely together that only their faces and elbows show.

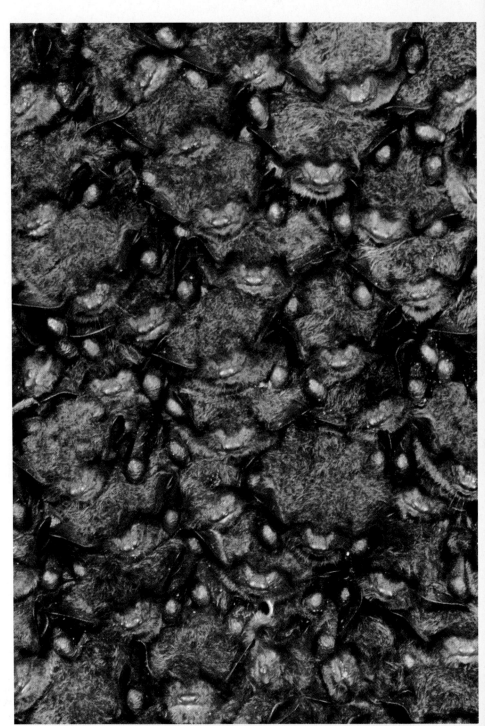

SKELETONS AREN'T SCARY

On Halloween, you'll probably see witches, ghosts and scary skeletons. Scary skeletons? Why in the world is a skeleton scary? You're around a skeleton every day—the one inside you.

All mammals, birds, fish, reptiles and amphibians have inner skeletons, too. Animals with an inner skeleton are called vertebrates and they all have backbones, rib cages, skulls and two pairs of limbs. But these parts aren't equally developed in every vertebrate. And if a part isn't well developed, the animal can't use it.

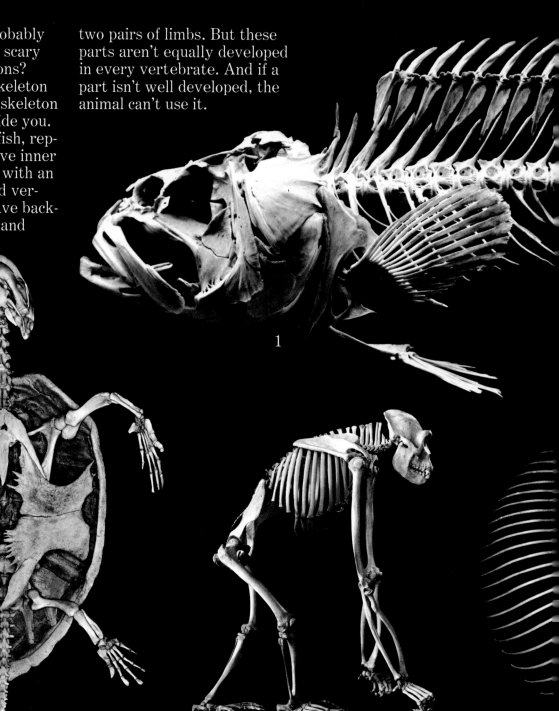

1

2

3

Let's look at some different skeletons and figure out what they have in common and how they're different.

With hundreds of bones, *fish* (1) have the most complex of all vertebrate skeletons. But their streamlined bodies only have the beginnings of arms and legs in the form of fins.

Turtles (2) have a special skeletal feature, too. Their rib cages and backbones are joined to an upper shell that protects their vital organs.

Like many vertebrates, their limbs connect to their body's trunk with "ball-and-socket" joints.

A *gorilla* skeleton (3) looks much like that of a man bending over. That's because they're both members of the same animal family, the primates.

A *snake* (4) may have as many as 300 small, interconnected bones, or vertebrae, in its backbone. (Man has 33 or 34.) All these joints help snakes to bend easily. And snakes can expand their rib cages and jaws to swallow prey twice their width.
EMILY MARSDEN

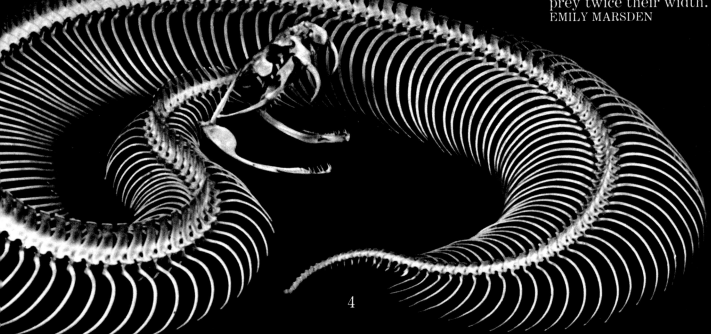

4

A SPOOKY NIGHT

Heartface flew to the edge of the high hayloft door on silent wings. It was time for her to go hunting with Tyto, her mate. Their nestlings, Hector and Fluff, were hungry and night was approaching fast. When Tyto joined her, the two barn owls flew off together.

Hector and Fluff were very comfortable in their home in the loft of the deserted barn. They were warm and dry and the chilly October weather didn't bother them. Soon their parents would return with food for their empty bellies.

The young owls scrunched down on the nest and listened to the soft sounds of the night. A twig snapped. The wind whispered through the leaves, and a small creature made rustling noises as it scampered through grass in the field outside.

Before long Hector closed his eyes and fell fast asleep. Fluff didn't feel at all sleepy. She was hungry and waited for her parents to return. She poked her head out of an opening in the barn and looked around. Soon the moon would come up, but now it was very dark. With her sharp eyesight, Fluff was able to see a nearby shed and a cluster of houses in the little village a short distance away.

Suddenly her sharp ears caught the *"ick-ick-ick"* of her mother's flight call. Fluff hopped back into the nest and bumped Hector. He opened his eyes and let out a hiss. Heartface moved toward her babies, who were calling for food with loud tittering sounds. She quickly stuffed the mouse she had brought them into their mouths.

Time passed. The days grew shorter and the weather colder, but Fluff and Hector were snug in their home. They grew quickly. Feathers the same color as their parents' gradually replaced their soft, white down. Tyto and Heartface were night hunters. Their keen hearing and eyesight made it easy for them to find food in the dark. Sometimes, though, when she was very hungry, Heartface would look for food during the day. One clear day she found an especially fat mouse. Her babies were well fed so she would enjoy this one herself. She swallowed it in one gulp.

On the very last night of October, Fluff was perched on the edge of one of the beams in the barn, looking out into the dark night. Lights glowed from the houses in the village, and a pale moon shone on the fields and trees. The young owl did not know it, but it was Halloween! It was a night for the village children to dress up in weird, spooky costumes and go

trick-or-treating." It was a
night for ghosts and goblins,
and the old barn that was Fluff
and Hector's home was supposed
to be haunted. When trick or
treating was over, what better
place for brave children to
visit than the crumbling barn?

From her perch, Fluff heard
noises coming from the barn
floor. Her head swung around
as she searched the darkness.
Instantly she saw strange creatures crouching and swaying
across the barn floor, making
soft, whispering sounds.

Suddenly one of the ghostly
creatures spotted Fluff. It
pointed at her and began to act
excitedly. Then the strange
figure started to climb a ladder
that reached toward Fluff's

perch high in the rafters.

Instinct told Fluff that something was wrong. She spread
her wings over her head and
hunched down. She started to
swing her head from side to side.
She hissed loudly and made
rapid clicking sounds with her
bill. All of this made her look
very fierce and dangerous.

The climber stopped. To see
better she pulled off her ghost
mask and dropped it.

"I'm going to catch you, owl,"
she called and moved another
few rungs up the ladder.

Fluff hissed and clicked and
flapped her wings. But she was

too young to fly away from the little girl.

Once again the climber stopped. She looked up at Fluff. The owl really did look fierce. Maybe she ought to leave the bird alone.

"Go on, Mary!" someone yelled up at her. "Go on!"

I'm scared." Mary called. "I'm coming down. You catch the owl if you want to!"

Just as Mary reached the barn floor, Heartface flew through the door. Her flight was swift and silent. None of the children heard or saw her.

Right away Heartface sensed that her baby was in trouble. Without a sound she swooped down toward the children like a small, white ghost. She did not touch them, but the children

began to scream excitedly.

Again and again Heartface dove at them. As she did, the frightened trick-or-treaters pushed and shoved each other out of the barn.

With the danger over, Heartface landed close to Fluff. "It's all right," she seemed to say. "It's all right."

LEE STOWELL CULLEN

INDEX

Illustrations are in **Boldface** type.

Africa: 20, 21, 51, 52, 55, 57
Albatross, wandering: 54, **54-55**
Ammonite: 7
Amphibian: 54, 88,
  largest, **54**, 55
Anaconda: 55, **54-55**
Animal: changing color, 63, 64
  color, 12, 13, 66, 68-69
  disguises, 60-69
  eyes, 20, 22, 35, 39, 51, 76-77, 80-81, **80-81**
  tails, **72-73**, 73
  tongues, 74-77, **74-77**
Ant: **36-37**, 44-45, **44-45**, 76
  harvester, **44-45**, 45
  honey, 45, **45**
  leaf cutter, 45, **45**
  tailor, 45, **45**
Antarctica: 24, 85
Anteater: 75-76, **76**
Aphid: 44-45, **44**
Asia: 20, 22-23, 55
Australia: 55, 73

Bacteria: 41
Bat: **84-87**, 85-86
  fruit, 85-86, **87**
  Indiana, 86, **86**
  little brown, 86, **86**
  vampire, **84-85**, 85
Bear: **14-15**
Bird: 59, 66-67, 88
  eye, **80**, 81
  heaviest flying, **54**, 55
  largest, 50-52, **50-53**, 54, **54**
  largest eggs, 54, **54**
  longest wingspan, 54, **54-55**
  nonflying, 24, **24-25**, 50-53, **50-53**, 54, **54**
Boa, emerald tree: 13
Brontosaurus: 13
Butterfly, gulf fritillary: 46, **46-47**

Camel: **18-21**, 19-21
Cat: 77
Caterpillar: gulf fritillary, 46, **46**
  spicebush swallowtail, 66-67, **67**
Centipede: 43
Chameleon: **74-75**, 75
  three-horned, **80**

Club moss: 10, **10**
Cobra, king: **80**
Coral snake, Arizona: 13
Coyote: **80**
Crocodile: **4-5**, 13, 59
  saltwater, 55, **55**

Dinosaur: 6, **12-13**
  color, 12-13
  skin, 12-13
  (see also *Fossils* and individual listings)
Dragonfly: 10

Eagle, bald: **80**
Echolocation: 85
Eel, moray: 64
Elephant: **48-49**, 54, 55

Fern: 10, **11**
Fish: largest, 54, **54-55**
  reef, **26-27**
  skeleton, 88-89, **88-89**
  (see also individual listings)
Fly: **38-39**, 39
Fossils: animal, 6-9, **8-9**, 12-13
  casts, 12-13
  "living," 10
Frog, flying: 22-23, **22-23**
  Goliath, **54**, 55
  largest, **54**, 55
  tongue, 75, **76**
  tree, 22-23, **22-23**, 81
Fungus: 41, 45

Gecko: 76-77, **76**, 81
Giraffe: **71**, 74-75, 75
Goldfish: **80**
Gorilla: **88**, 89
Ground pine: 10, **10**

Hippopotamus: **56-59**, 57-59
Horsetail: 10

Ichthyosaur: 6-9, **6-9**
Insect: 59, 66

Jellyfish: lion's mane, 35, **35**
  moon, 35
  Polyorchus, **34**, 35

Kangaroo: 73, **73**
Komodo dragon: 13, **54**, 55
Kori bustard: **54**, 55

Lemming: **60-61**
Leopard: 77, **77**
Lion: 59
Liverwort: 10, **10**
Lizard: 13
  gecko, 76-77, **76**, 81
  Komodo dragon, **54**, 55

largest, **54**, 55
Lorikeet, rainbow: **80**

Mammal: 88
  eyes, 81
  flying, 85
  largest, 54, **54-55**
Mantis, praying: 66, **66-67**
Megatherium: 17
"Mermaid's purse": 29
Millipede: 43
Mold, slime: 43
Monkey: **80**
  squirrel, **81**
Moss, sphagnum: 10, **10**
Moth: 69, **69**
  Io, 67, **67**
  Polyphemus, **80**
Mouse: **90**, 91

Narwhal: 78, **78-79**

Octopus: 63-65, **62-65**
Ostrich: 50-52, **50-53**, 54, **54**
Owl: 67
  barn, **90-93**, 91-93
  fish, **81**
Oxpecker: **70-71**

Penguin, Adélie: 24, **24-25**
Pig: **81**
Plankton: 30, 54
Plesiosaur: 9
Porcupine fish: 32, **33**
Porpoise: 29
Pseudoscorpion: 41, 43
Ptarmigan: 69, **69**
Pterodactyl: 9
Puffer fish: 32, **32**
Python, reticulated: **54-55**, 55

Rabbit, cottontail: **81**
Rabies: 86
Raccoon: **1**, 3, **81**
Rattlesnake: 73, **73**
Reptile: 13, 54, 88, **88-89**
  largest, 55, **55**

Scorpion fish, spotted: 68, 69
Sea horse: **80**
Seal, leopard: 24
Shark: 28-31, **28-31**, 32
  basking, 30
  blacktip, 31, **31**
  blue, **30**, 31,
  epaulette, 31, **31**
  great white, **28-29**, 29
  horn, 31, **31**
  largest, 54, **54-55**
  nurse, 31, **31**
  whitetip, reef, 30, **31**
  whale, 30, 54, **54-55**

Skeleton: **8-9**, 9, 88-89, **88-89**
  (see also *Fossils*)
Sloth: three-toed, **16-17**, 17
  two-toed, 17
Snail: 41
Snake: 13, **88-89**, 89
  heaviest, **54-55**, 55
  longest, **54-55**, 55
  (see also individual listings)
South America: 17, 55
Sowbug: 41
Sphagnum moss: 10, **10**
Spider: jumping, **38-39**, 39
  wolf, 43
Springtail: 41
Squirrel, flying: 85
Swimbladder: 31

Tail: **72-73**, 73
Tick: 59, **70-71**
Tiger: **80**
Toad: 75
Tongue: 74-77, **74-77**
Turkey: **72**, 73
Turtle: **88**, 89
  box, **81**
  largest, **54**, 55
  leatherback sea, **54**, 55
Tyrannosaurus rex: 6, **12-13**, 13

Unicorn: 78, **78-79**

Vertebrates: 88-89, **88-89**

Walking stick: 68, 69
Whale: 64
  blue, 54, **54-55**
  killer, 29
  narwhal, 78, **78-79**
Woodpecker: 76, **76**
Wrasse: **81**

Zebra: 13, 52

Library of Congress Cataloging in Publication Data

Main entry under title:

Ranger Rick's surprise book.

  Includes index.
  SUMMARY: Contains articles and activities compiled from Ranger Rick's nature magazine focusing on unusual aspects of nature.
  1. Zoology—Miscellanea—Juvenile literature.
[1. Zoology—Miscellanea]
I. Ranger Rick's nature magazine.

QL49.R35   591   79-88095
ISBN 0-912186-32-1

ILLUSTRATION CREDITS

TEXT CREDITS

The Editors wish to thank the editorial staff of *Ranger Rick's Nature Magazine* for permission to present the following selections:

Surprises from Ages Past
"Mary and the Monster," March 1974.
"Living Fossils," October 1976.
"Dinosaurs in Technicolor," July 1975.

Surprises Around the World
"It's Speedy Sloth," March 1972.
"Stuck Together Beast," April 1976.
"The Adélies of Antarctica," December 1971.

Surprises Beneath the Sea
"Sharks," January 1977.
"The Puffer Is a Bluffer," July 1972.
"Saucers of the Sea," August 1977.

Surprises in Tiny Places
"It's the Little Jumping Spider," November 1971.
"Watch Out for Mini-Monsters," April 1978.
"The Amazing Ant," April 1974.
"Butterfly Magic," June 1978.

Surprises in Big Sizes
"Big Bird," July 1975.
"How Big Is Big?" February 1975.
"The Fat Ones," December 1976.

Surprises in Disguises
"The Secret World of the Octopus," April 1976.
"Acting Fierce," based on "Nature's Bag of Tricks, Trick 2," February 1974; and "Who-o-o Knows?" September 1977.
"Four Disappearing Acts," based on "Nature's Bag of Tricks, Trick 1," November 1973; "Nature's Bag of Tricks, Trick 3," July 1974; and "Scorpion of the Sea," June 1978.

Surprises from Head to Tail
"Tale of Tails," May/June 1975.
"Tricky Tongues," October 1975.
"The Unicorn Was a Narwhal," January 1976.
"Who's Looking at You?" based on "Eyes," February 1973.

Surprises for a Stormy Night
"Bats," October 1975.
"Skeletons Aren't Scary," October 1971.
"A Spooky Night," October 1975.

The editors also appreciate the opportunity to present "Flying Frogs," copyright ©1977 by Mary Leister. Reprinted by permission of Stemmer House Publishers, Inc., Owings Mills, Maryland.

National Wildlife Federation

1412 16th Street, N.W.
Washington, D.C.
20036

Thomas L. Kimball, *Executive Vice President*
J. A. Brownridge, *Administrative Vice President*
James D. Davis, *Director, Book Development*

Staff for this Book

Elizabeth G. Jones
Editor

Nancy Birch Halperin
Art Editor

David M. Seager
Art Director

Robyn Gregg
Editorial Assistant

Mel Baughman
Production Manager

Mariam Thayer Rutter
Production Artist

Cathy Pelletier
Permissions Editor

Acknowledgments

The editors are especially grateful to the staff of the National Wildlife Federation's *Ranger Rick's Nature Magazine* for the creative and challenging way they have encouraged children's involvement in the natural world. The articles and stories published during the magazine's history provided the incentive as well as the rich resource from which this book grew.

The editorial staff also feel fortunate to have worked with illustrator Roz Schanzer, who contributed both her ideas and talents to help create the mazes which introduce each chapter.

While the editors received generous assistance from many NWF colleagues, we would like to give special thanks to National Wildlife naturalists Craig Tufts and Susan Ennett and wildlife biologist William S. Clark. Thanks are also due the personnel at the Smithsonian Museum of Natural History and reference librarians at the Library of Congress and Fairfax (Virginia) Public Library for their interest and assistance with this book.